Catastrophes in India's Social Landscape

About the Editors

Dr. Joyashri Dey (MSW (Gold Medalist), PhD, UGC-NET & JRF) is Assistant Professor, Department of Social Work, Assam (A Central) University, Silchar, India. She has pursued her Post Graduation and Doctoral Research from Assam (A Central) University, Silchar. She has an experience of working with many regional and national level reputed NGOs including Oxfam International, Kolkata, HLFPPT, Delhi. She has been the Editor of a book of the title "Globalization and the Concerns of Social Landscape in India". She has also published several research articles in various reputed national and international journals and also chapters in several edited books.

Mr. Rajdeep Dutta (MSW (Gold Medalist), MA (Edu), UGC-NET & JRF) is Non-Medical Faculty (MSW), Department of Community Medicine, Tezpur Medical College & Hospital. He is also a Ph.D. Candidate at the Department of Social Work, Assam (A Central) University, Silchar, India. He has pursued his Post Graduation in MSW from Assam (A Central) University, Silchar and MA (Edu) from Krishna Kanta Handiqui State Open University, Guwahati, Assam. In his academic career, he has published his research works in various reputed national and international journals and also chapters for edited books. He has also contributed his research papers in many National & International Conferences.

Acknowledgements

Our philosophy is that knowledge expands through sharing. In bringing this volume of the book before the readers, first, we would like to express our gratitude to the contributory authors who took the time and effort to prepare and write a chapter for the book and meant to contribute their academic research work through this volume. Your input is not confined just to widening academic understanding, but it will consciously draw the attention of policy makers in framing associated initiatives to change and bring development.

Additionally, we would like to express our gratitude to our colleagues, well-wishers, and everybody who has assisted us in any way, whether directly or indirectly, in bringing this book to completion.

We are also appreciative of our respective institutions for supporting and inspiring us in different ways. Finally, we would like to express our heartfelt gratitude to the publisher, "Concept Publishing House", for accepting our proposal and cooperating with us to bring this volume to reality.

Joyashri Dey
Rajdeep Dutta

Preface

We all are well known for the fact that how COVID-19 has affected our lives in almost all the segments including all the groups of population. COVID-19 has posed a serious threat to the lives of the people, economy and society. The abrupt and extremely harsh response to COVID-19 pandemic in India has aggravated social and economic deprivations and inequalities. With each passing day in the unprecedented crisis situation around COVID-19 pandemic, India has espoused to pre-existing inequalities and injustices that have been laid out around us. These inevitably have a serious adverse impact on different facets of human life. COVID-19 crisis and the "lockdown" has worst impact in terms of workload and reduced economic opportunities, lack of access to health facilities, nutrition and increase in incidence of gender-based violence, communalization and racialization along with stigma associated with COVID-19.

The volume of this edited book is to shed light on the major catastrophes that outbreak in the education, health, and other underprivileged sectors of India's socio-economic landscape during and post-COVID-19 pandemic. The edited volume of this book has eighteen different chapters divided into three distinct sections. **Section-I** has focused on the theme 'COVID-19, Education and Technology' consisting of three papers, **Section-II** has focused on the theme 'COVID-19 and Health' consisting of six papers, and **Section-III** has focused on the theme 'COVID-19 and its Impact on Marginalised Groups' with nine papers. Therefore, the book is an updated version which contains varied information about COVID-19 and it impacts in India that shared by the contributors through their diversity of work, insights, and perspectives will be beneficial at large. In this way, this edited book will certainly contribute knowledge and will draw the attention of policymakers, academicians, activists, practitioners, and for further research and practice.

Joyashri Dey
Rajdeep Dutta

ISBN: 978-93-5594-523-5

First Published 2023

Published and Printed by

Concept Since 1974

Concept Publishing Company Pvt. Ltd.
A/15-16, Commercial Block, Mohan Garden,
New Delhi-110059 (India)
T: +91-11-41101460
E : publishing@conceptpub.com, *W*: www.conceptpub.com

Cataloging in Publication Data–Courtesy: D.K. Agencies (P) Ltd. <docinfo@dkagencies.com>

Catastrophes in India's social landscape : its society and COVID-19 pandemic / edited by Joyashri Dey, Rajdeep Dutta.
pages cm
Contributed articles.
Includes bibliographical references and index.
ISBN 9789355945235

1. COVID-19 Pandemic, 2020- --Social aspects--India. 2. COVID-19 Pandemic, 2020- --India--Psychological aspects. 3. Women--India--Social conditions. 4. Marginality, Social--India. I. Dey, Joyashri, editor. II. Dutta, Rajdeep, editor.

LCC RA644.C67C38 2023 | DDC 362.196241400954 23

Catastrophes in India's Social Landscape

Its Society and COVID-19 Pandemic

Edited by
Joyashri Dey
Rajdeep Dutta

CONCEPT PUBLISHING COMPANY PVT. LTD.
NEW DELHI-110059

Contents

SECTION-III

COVID-19 AND ITS IMPACT ON MARGINALISED GROUPS

List of Contributors

Ms. Asha B.N., Research Scholar, Department of Political Science, Karnatak University, Dharwad, Karnataka. Email: ashabn1012kai@gmail.com

Ms. Anjali Thakur, Operations Manager, Shakti Shalini, New Delhi. Email: anjali.thakur@shaktishalini.org

Ms. Anns Mariya, II MSW, Dept. of Social Work, Kristu Jayanti College, Bangalore, Karnataka. Email: annsmariajose98@gmail.com

Ms. Archana, II MSW, Dept. of Social Work, Kristu Jayanti College, Bangalore, Karnataka. Email: archanasnair1106@gmail.com

Ms. B. Preethi Meena, Employability Coordinator, Diya Foundation, Bangalore, Karnataka. Email: preethi@diyafoundation-india.org

Ms. Bhaswati Borah, Assistant Professor, NEF Law College, Guwahati, Assam. Email: bhaswati.baruah18@gmail.com

Dr. Bijoy Das, Assistant Professor, Programme of Social Work, Faculty of Humanities and Social Sciences, Assam down town University, Guwahati, Assam. Email: das.bijoy96@gmail.com

Dr. Dipsikha Das, Assistant Professor, Department of Economics, S.M. Dev College, Lakhipur, Cachar, Assam. Email: dasdipsikha2010@ rediffmail.com

Dr. Gadigeppa M. Sunagar, Assistant Professor, KSS Vijayanagar College of Education, and P.G. Center of Studies in Education, Vidyanagar, Hubli, Karnataka. Email: girishsunagar@gmail.com

Ms. Gigin Mariya, II MSW, Dept. of Social Work, Kristu Jayanti College, Bangalore, Karnataka. Email: giginmariya98@gmail.com

Ms. Irin Theresa, II MSW, Dept. of Social Work, Kristu Jayanti College, Bangalore, Karnataka. Email: irinalappat@gmail.com

Dr. Joyashri Dey, Assistant Professor, Department of Social Work, Assam (A Central) University, Silchar, Assam. Email: joyasreedey1@gmail.com

Dr. Kasturi Bora, Assistant Professor, NEF Law College, Guwahati, Assam. Email: search4kasturi@gmail.com

Mr. Kshetrimayum Dayananda Singh, Ph.D. Scholar, Department of Social Work, Assam University, Silchar, Assam. Email: lamjingg@ gmail.com.

Dr Karavi Barman, Assistant Professor, NEF Law College, affiliated to Guwahati University, Guwahati, Assam. Email: karavi78@gmail.com

Mr. Lovepreet Singh, Project Analyst, Quality Council of India, New Delhi. Email: love.chahal23@gmail.com.

Ms. Mercy Hazarika, Assistant Professor, Department of Social Work, Mahapurusha Srimanta Sankaradeva Viswavidyalaya, Guwahati, Assam. Email: mercshy17@gmail.com

Ms. Priyanka Gogoi, Assistant Professor, Department of Social Work, Mahapurusha Srimanta Sankaradeva Viswavidyalaya, Guwahati, Assam. Email: priyank.gogoi3@gmail.com

Ms. Priya Mondal, Research Scholar, Department of Education, Assam University, Silchar, Assam. Email: priyamondal90@gmail.com

Ms. Pragya Sharma, Institute of Home Economics, University of Delhi, Hauz Khas, New Delhi. Email: sharma.pragya7596@gmail.com

Ms. Puja Sorong, M.Phil. Research Scholar, Department of Education, Dibrugarh University, Hojai, Assam, India. Email: sorongpuja@gmail.com

Mr. Rajdeep Dutta, UGC-Senior Research Fellow (Ph.D. Candidate), Department of Social Work, Assam (A Central) University, Silchar, Assam. Email: duttaraj9864@gmail.com

Ms. Shilpi Sikha Das, Ph.D. Candidate, Centre of Social Medicine and Community Health (CSMCH), Jawaharlal Nehru University, New Delhi. Email: shilpisikha.das@gmail.com

Mr. Somodatta Bhattacharjee, Research Scholar, Department of History, Assam University, Silchar, Assam. Email: somodattab31@gmail.com

Dr. Shan Eugene Palakkal, Assistant Professor, Department of History and Tourism, Stella Maris College (Autonomous) 17, Cathedral Road, Chennai, Tamil Nadu. Email: shan.eugene@gmail.com

Ms. Shemi Saji, II MSW, Dept. of Social Work, Kristu Jayanti College, Bangalore, Karnataka. Email: shemishaji99@gmail.com

Dr. Swapan Banerjee, Department of Nutrition, Seacom Skills University, Kendradangal-731236, Birbhum, West Bengal. Email: dieticianbanerjee@gmail.com

Mr. Sandip Sutradhar, Research Scholar, Tezpur University, Hojai, Assam. Email: sandipsutradhar009@gmail.com

Ms. Tanmoyee Bhattacharjee, Project Co-ordinator, Shakti Shalini, New Delhi. Email: bhattacharjee.tanmayee@gmail.com

Dr Winnie Joyce A., Assistant Professor, Dept. of Social Work, Kristu Jayanti College, Bangalore, Karnataka. Email: winniejoyce@kristujayanti.com

Introduction

COVID-19 has unleashed unprecedented economic and social hardship around the world. The abrupt and extremely harsh response to COVID-19 pandemic in India has aggravated social and economic deprivations and inequalities. With each passing day in the unprecedented crisis situation around COVID-19 pandemic, India has espoused to pre-existing inequalities and injustices that have been laid out around us. These inevitably have a serious adverse impact on different facets of human life. COVID-19 crisis and the "lockdown" has worst impact in terms of workload and reduced economic opportunities, lack of access to health facilities, nutrition and increase in incidence of gender-based violence, communalization and racialization along with stigma associated with COVID.

The purpose of this volume is to shed light on the major catastrophes that outbreak in the education, health, and other underprivileged sectors of India's socio-economic landscape during and post the COVID-19 pandemic. The edited volume of this book has eighteen different chapters divided into three distinct sections. Section-I has focused on the theme 'COVID-19, Education and Technology' consisting of three papers, Section-II has focused on the theme 'COVID-19 and Health' consisting of six papers, and Section-III has focused on the theme 'COVID-19 and its Impact on Marginalised Groups' with nine papers.

This volume started with the discussion on "Information and Communication Technology (ICT) and Its Impact on Education during and Post-COVID-19 Period" by **Ms. Puja Sorong and Mr. Sandip Sutradhar.** The article highlighted that the prevailing situation has become challenging due to COVID-19. But with the help of ICT, we can cope with the situation and it plays a very significant role in the field of education. ICT allows accessing a variety of information sources within minutes. This research paper is basically descriptive and analytical in nature. The major result of the study found that ICT can enable teachers to transform their teaching practices. ICTs are seen as important tools to enable and support the move from traditional 'teaching-centric' teaching styles to more learner-centric methods. In this particular paper, the researchers have also tried to discuss the expected opportunities and structural changes in the post-COVID-19 education system in India.

Covering the "COVID-19 and Its Repercussions on the Cyber Security Landscape" **Dr. Shan Eugene Palakkal** shed light on how pandemics affect cyber security issues and the increase in cyber-attacks targeting vulnerable sections of society. The pandemic and the imposed lockdown have led people to be confined to their homes for hours, spending time on the internet. The dangers of cyber-crime have been lurking there for a long time, but with the increase in the population connected to the internet and the time spent online, along with a sense of confinement, anxiety, and fear, there has been an increase in opportunities for cyber-criminals to take advantage of such situations. It is the most vulnerable section of society, like children, adolescents, and women, who spend time online for schooling, learning, and other creative talents. The elderly, who usually rely on offline shopping, are now relying on the internet and they too, equally, find themselves exposed to cyber-crime.

COVID-19 has been declared a "pandemic" by the World Health Organization (WHO) that is causing serious damage to human existence globally. This virus has been effective in forcing a nationwide shutdown of a variety of tasks, notably academic shows, and, due to this, many schools are leaving their normal geographic locations and opting for virtual learning platforms. **Mr. Rajdeep Dutta and Dr. Joyashri Dey** in their article opined on "Schools Lock but Classes Unlock: Virtual Learning for School Children during the COVID-19 Pandemic" how the crisis strategies adopted by educational institutions, teaching staff, and school children, are met with numerous challenges and opportunities, and how online learning is distinct from obstacles and an alternative in the educational paradigm in times of global emergency. Accordingly, the current research also identifies suggestions for both school administrators and teachers as well as for students with regard to virtual teaching-learning contexts.

Considering the significant area of COVID-19 and mental health, **Dr. Bijoy Das** in his reviewed paper "COVID-19 and Its Impact on the Mental Health of the Elderly" tries to explore the possible mental health challenges that are faced by the elderly in this outbreak of COVID-19. We are all well known for the fact that how COVID-19 has affected our lives in almost all the segments, including all the groups of the population. Studies have witnessed that, due to the age factor and the low immunity system of the elderly, this group has become the most vulnerable to this deadly disease. As a result, they are suffering from various mental illnesses like stress, anxiety, insomnia, depression, etc. These are all due to the excess of information provided on the TV channels about the death toll and the vulnerability of this age group. Besides, the matter of social distance and fear of isolation have all become important factors in rising tensions among the group rather than giving importance to physical distance.

Simultaneously, covering mental health, a vital ailment, **Mr. Kshetrimayum Dayananda Singh** in his article opined on understanding the risk factors leading to the cause of mental stress during the pandemic and the role of the government in controlling mental stress during the nationwide lockdown. The new normal in the form of lockdown, social distancing norms, shifting from physical attendance to workplace and educational institutions to online mode, and restrictions on immigration have become an integral part of the day-to-day lives of people. It is universally accepted that in order to fight the COVID-19 deadly virus, people should religiously follow the norms endorsed by medical experts around the world, as a result of which many precious human lives have been saved. At the same time, adequate attention is also sought to effectively address the issue of mental health problems triggered by the fear of getting infected with the deadly disease and the adoption of such strict measures.

In the article titled, "Stress and Emotional Responses of Dakshin Dinajpur in West Bengal as a Result of the COVID-19 Pandemic: A Mixed-Method Analysis", **Ms. Priya Mondal** reflects on how human behaviour has evolved and how internal and external influences, such as personality characteristics, gender, the media, the economy, and government response, affect the social understanding of the pandemic and the psychological outcomes of the current situation. Furthermore, we looked at populations that are at a higher risk of mental health problems as a result of these circumstances. Health care workers, seniors, infants, college students, economically poor people, the homeless, inmates, the rural population, and psychiatric patients are included in this situation. We also spoke about several strategies for reducing the emotional effects of this situation. Health officials, the community, and the general public must work together to assist disadvantaged groups and encourage emotional and psychological support.

To highlight and analyze maternal health and its mental, social, and psychological challenges in India during the COVID-19 scenario, **Dr. Swapan Banerjee and Ms. Pragya Sharma** in their article tried to discuss how pregnant women are often neglected during gestation, childbirth, and even postpartum periods living under the poorer sections and lower-middle-class families in India, like in developing countries. The level of distress in healthcare, nutrition, and total care during the COVID-19 phases has increased. The study analyzed and showed that pregnant mothers in low to lower-income groups always suffer in all aspects, and the COVID-19 phases increased that pain much more. Hence, better infrastructure and prompt medical facilities at low cost are required for them because they are the carriers of their children and the respect of a nation.

Teachers play an important and influential role in the lives of their students, and, in many cases, their families and the community. Their duties and responsibilities extend far beyond meeting learning outcomes, to caring for the social and emotional needs of their students. But who's looking out for our teachers? To address the issue, **Dr. Gadigeppa M. Sunagar** in the article highlighted that the health and safety of teachers and their families must be a priority as they try to balance the different demands of work and home. COVID-19 has shed light on the important role that teachers play in supporting students' learning and well-being. Adapting to new and sometimes uncertain situations and events, is not an uncommon feature in the lives of teachers, like dealing with unexpected student behaviour, teaching classes with different student levels and abilities, and making adjustments to timetables and lesson plans as a result of curriculum changes. In fact, their role requires adaptability regularly to navigate the demands of their everyday work in schools and classrooms.

The COVID-19 pandemic and lockdown have exaggerated reproductive health services such as maternal health, family planning, and abortion services in India. To find out the impact of the lockdown on the COVID-19 pandemic on the mental health of pregnant women in the Barak Valley, **Dr. Dipsikha Das** presented her opinion from different news reports that pregnant women were worried about the life security of newborn babies. Different kinds of thoughts are coming into their minds regarding their health as well as their infant. Actually, this pandemic affects maternal health more, especially the mental health of pregnant women. The findings state that depression is the most common problem among pregnant women due to an uncertain situation. The lack of health services and the increasing number of home deliveries without the assistance of trained health workers amplify the stress and depression problems among these women. Though the government is trying to provide the facilities, for several reasons, mental health status cannot be improved up to the mark.

To understand the lives of working women during the pandemic from a gender perspective, **Ms. Priyanka Gogoi and Ms. Mercy Hazarika** in their article cited that household work is thought to be the sole responsibility of females, hence work-life balance is already challenging for women. COVID-19 is a novel coronavirus reported first by the Wuhan Municipal Health Commission, China, that was declared as a pandemic by the World Health Organisation (WHO) on 11th March, 2020. In a very short period, the virus has spread globally and it has affected the world in the socio-economic and political spheres. In India, the first case of COVID-19 was detected in Kerala and as the number of cases increased nationally, a national lockdown was announced on 23rd March, 2020 to stop the further spread. People were strictly ordered to stay at home and hence had to adapt to working from home. Thus, using qualitative research, this study was an attempt to understand working women's lives during the COVID-19 lockdown in Guwahati city.

Violence against women, also known as gender-based violence, is certainly the dark feature of the pandemic and the mirror of the image, as it is an omnipresent element of society and existed even before the pandemic, fostering attention not only in the state but worldwide. To address the issues, **Dr. Karavi Barman** in her article shared the opinion that feminine privacy often militates the man's right to castle. Violence against women is at its peak and it has left its permanent footprints, leading to insecurities in all forms. The deep paradox lies imbedded in structural violence. This period is an opportunity to rethink the parameters of constitutional jurisprudence. The paper is a humble attempt to showcase the concepts of self-respect, self-determination, and self-autonomy of a woman juggling to find her place in the welfare state. The researcher has also provided an insight into the Domestic Violence Act to obviate the possibility of disruption to the carefully crafted constitutional practices and conventions.

Covering the impact of COVID-19 on social inequalities and gender, **Ms. Asha B.N.** in her article tries to highlight the different realities that women could be facing in light of this pandemic and to raise awareness about some of the social inequality and gender impacts that COVID-19 is having on our society. COVID-19 compounding risks to progress towards gender equality, the pandemic and its consequences hit the world economy harder than ever before and are having a deep effect on human development, and it is also affecting several social, economic, and political dimensions of women. Across every phase of life, from health to the economy, and security to social protection, gender-based violence, the impact of COVID-19 is exacerbated for women and simply by virtue of their sex. India needs to avoid this. It must leverage female agencies and it needs to adopt more gender-inclusive policy planning and implementation to manage the COVID-19 pandemic crisis.

To put forth some business solutions for pandemic challenges, the authors, **Dr. Kasturi Bora and Ms. Bhaswati Borah,** have studied the various challenges faced by various business sectors in India due to COVID-19 and labour migration. An unprecedented large-scale reverse migration of labour triggered by the nationwide lockdown, that saw millions of workers travel across state borders, has put some of the Indian economy's biggest sectors at risk. The lockdown, which was then extended twice, hit millions of daily wage earners and migrant labourers who were left without jobs and income. Penniless and stranded, workers left cities for their villages on foot or bicycles, cramped in trucks and later by trains. The result is a labour crunch which might hit capacity utilisation for several firms. Manufacturing is the obvious victim of its high reliance on migrants. Companies that have manufacturing facilities in multiple states are better hedged against labour scarcity.

Socially and economically marginalized communities experience excruciating suffering due to highly segmented settlements and the prevailing deprived living conditions. To address these issues, authors **Mr. Lovepreet Singh, Ms. Tanmoyee Bhattacharjee, and Ms. Anjali Thakur,** shared their opinion that urban marginalised communities, mainly comprise daily wage earners, migrant labourers, and domestic workers with highly volatile sources of income, leaving them in extreme financial distress. The outbreak of the virus followed by the nationwide lockdown resulted in the loss of livelihood, food scarcity, furthered by poor healthcare infrastructure, and inaccessibility to education because of a wide digital gap. Increased household distress and incidents of domestic violence were reported, primarily affecting women and children, given the social structure in such communities. The survey primarily focused on measuring the impact of the COVID-19 pandemic on economic conditions/employment, food scarcity, and lack of resources to access digital education.

The article by **Dr. Winnie Joyce A. and others** has enlightened views about how the current global pandemic has increased the outbreak of domestic violence in India due to the financial crisis. The study shows that by examining the location of the incidents, most of the violence issues are reported from the northern part of the nation. The victims are mostly from the Hindu religion. The consequences faced by the family differ from case to case. But in an overall view, the husband's family is not treating the victim as well as the spouses. Different kinds of exploitation are faced by females as many of them are treated like slaves who are tied tightly under the marriage knot as they lack the freedom to enjoy the outer world. Lack of education is also the reason behind this. Most of the issues are from rural areas of the nation. Women's empowerment can help these youths to escape from these dilemmas to an extent, as they can enable themselves to stand on their own feet in the world.

In the changing dynamics of 'Home' as a social institution during COVID-19, **Ms. Shilpi Sikha Das,** in her inscription, cited that the pandemic has been deconstructing the nature of social institutions and their functionality. The interplay of various social institutions maintains societal equilibrium. The pandemic introduced restrictions on movement and social gathering, thus making all the social institutions freeze, except the family in a household. The study would use 'home' and 'household' instead of 'family' as a social institute, considering the demands and expectations of households as a unit during the pandemic. "Stay at Home" has been a strong preventive measure advocated to flatten the curve of the pandemic. The study aims to highlight the pre and during pandemic roles of the home as a social institution. The major themes to be explored are healthcare, well-being, food security, education, employment, protection, and security. The focus of the study is to explore and understand Indian homes during the pandemic, which opens up the study to a multidimensional understanding based on diversity.

Looking at the impact of COVID-19 on women's lives, **Mr. Somodatta Bhattacharjee** in his article described how the world has been in complete disorder since the outbreak of the deadly viral infection, COVID-19. It has rapidly infected millions globally. Like many other countries across the globe, on 22nd March, 2020, a nationwide lockdown was declared in India. When we hear of a lockdown, our attention is shifted to the visible problems associated with it, like health hazards, economic slowdown, migrant issues, and others. But if we look a little closely, an entirely separate power dynamics is also associated with it, and this is the adverse effect of the pandemic lockdown on women. This study will attempt to understand the impact of the pandemic and the resultant lockdown on women, how they were subjected to domestic violence, extreme workload, and how the pandemic affected them physically and mentally. Attempts are also made to look into the new opportunities which have come up in the situation and suggestions are also made to deal with the pandemic situation.

In describing the stress and challenges experienced by the parents of individuals with multiple disabilities during the

COVID-19 pandemic, **Ms. B. Preethi Meena** presented the opinion that individuals with multiple disabilities are among the most affected communities during this pandemic. Young adults with multiple disabilities are much more prone to risk due to their vulnerability and to unexpected complex changes. The pandemic has not only disrupted the lives of people with multiple disabilities but also their families, especially their parents. Major factors like the sudden loss of job, financial inefficiency, inability to satisfy basic needs, and the restrictions of lockdown and home quarantine add to the causes of mental stress for parents. The researcher also suggested some of the remedies and strategies made and used by the Diya Foundation during COVID-19 and how its interventions have benefited the respondents. With this background, the paper also underlines the implications of future research and practice.

We end with the expectation that the diversity of work, insights, and perspectives given and shared by the writers would be extremely beneficial and may attract the attention of policymakers, academicians, activists, practitioners, and researchers to further studies, practice, and opportunities.

Joyashri Dey
Rajdeep Dutta

SECTION-I

COVID-19, EDUCATION AND TECHNOLOGY

1
Information and Communication Technology (ICT) and Its impact on Education during and the Post-COVID-19 Period

Puja Sorong and *Sandip Sutradhar*

Introduction

Information technology is a type of technology which performs various types of activities such as collecting, sorting, processing, retrieving, using and transmitting, these informations with maximum accuracy and efficiency in enriching the knowledge of the user in decision making within minimum time. Information technology shares and interchanges knowledge, mental skills, motor skills and attitudes etc. among the users through the use of electronic mass media. Communication means exchanging ideas or information through sending messages or otherwise. Dewy defines communication as a process of sharing experiences to modify the disposition of both. *(M.K. Gowswami)*. During this pandemic situation, it becomes difficult to teach or take classes as before. Now ICT has become one of the strongest medium to continue the educational process. ICTs can present content in an engaging and attractive form in education to the learner. ICT helps the teachers to record and constantly monitor the progress of each student. It allows customized delivery of relevant education material to each individual learner. It can build virtual social communities among different educational institutions, teams of teachers and students. It provides the opportunity to facilitate learning-to-learn skills. The latest innovations in ICTs (mobile tools, cloud solutions, etc.) allow to implement continuous learning processes in different learning contexts and provide on-demand support to students.

Objectives of the Study

- To study the impact of ICT on education during COVID-19.
- To analyze the effect of ICT in teaching learning process during COVID-19.
- To study about the opportunities and changes in the field of education in post-COVID-19 period in India.
- To study about the long-term impact of Digital learning in education sector in post-COVID-19 period in India.

Methodology of the Study

This chapter is basically descriptive and analytical in nature. The data used in it is purely from secondary sources according to the need of the study. Information collected from the publications of the Journals, Articles, Books and the Educational websites, are extensively used.

Review of Literature

According to UNESCO 2020, on 9 April, 2020, there are over 1,50,00,00,000 learners worldwide from primary to tertiary class who cannot attend in educational institutions. Due to enormous and immediate closures, influenced nations and societies have been compelled to set up hasty fixes in various digital learning platforms. These quick actions from classroom to online education have committed more serious inquiries associated with national educational policies and academic grounds and theories. Existing situations of traditional academic strategies can be interpreted utilizing Philip Strong's (1990) model of epidemic psychology comprising of 3 straight and coinciding epidemics: those of fear, justification, and effort. Strong employs 'epidemic' as an analogy exemplifying united psychological responses to an epidemiological problem. Selwyn (2020) had mentioned that these preferences can potentially reflect in the future as modern connections of energy and control, recent aspects of learner disservice and imbalance, and different uncertain consequences. In order to mitigate feasible adverse effects, academic institutions should influence the earlier understanding of online learning as something that can be better differed than only a means to provide data. Bourdieu (1984) had mentioned that they are in problem of receding into the tangle of particular B misrecognition (see that is, into comprehending digital learning as a self-evident and all-encompassing treatment to the further profound difficulties of existing mass education and institutionalized education).

Importance of the Study

The present scenario of the world is very pathetic, thousands and lacs of peoples are dying daily. The situation become quite abnormal, particularly students are not able to get their education as before. But if there is problem, the solutions are also hiding behind the problem, now ICT become one of the strongest alternatives to educate our learner and continue our educational system. ICTs are impacting on the content of education curricula stems from the ways in which ICTs have become essential part of our learning system. Realizing the significance of planning, re-constructing and modifying the present education structure, curriculum, academic session etc. for post-COVID-19 era due certain changes as well as development of new opportunities in the field of education, the researcher desire to make a humble attempt to study about the importance of ICT in education during and post-COVID-19 era in India.

Findings

- **To study the impact of ICT on education during COVID-19:** The Education system has changed with new form in all levels of education during the COVID-19 period. In this ongoing pandemic virtual education has become a norm for most of the educational institutions in our country. With the need to contain the virus, many countries are implementing measures to reduce gatherings of large crowds. Our schools are not immune to these actions, or to the spread of the virus. Many countries have now implemented measures in their education systems – from banning gatherings to the temporary closing of schools. Now ICT is only the alternative to continue our education. The ICT has great impact on education; it makes education easier than the traditional learning system. It makes the education more learner-centred. The prevailing situation becomes very challenging and difficult due to COVID-19. But with the help of ICT, we can cope up with the situation in a very efficient manner. ICT plays a very significant role in the field of education. ICT gives the opportunity to access the variety of information sources within minute. It becomes easy to communicate with students from any place, any time with the help of ICT.

- **To analyze the effect of ICT in teaching learning process during COVID-19:** The COVID-19 pandemic has adversely disrupted various sectors of education which is a critical determinant of a country's economic future. In India, the state governments across the country began to shut down the educational institutions temporarily as a measure to contain the spread of the COVID-19. COVID-19 pandemic has impacted on the various aspects of Indian education sector such as structure of educational institutions, teaching method, assessment, methodology, pedagogical method, courses etc. Due to COVID-19 more than 180 million school children are staying home. But while schools are temporarily closed for quarantine, schooling continues. It's just that it is a different kind of teaching. Students are being educated remotely using technology. This is being done through a variety of online courses and electronic textbooks. The effectiveness of ICTs on teaching learning system is positive but the acceptability is very challengeable in India though we are habituated to learn in traditional teaching learning method. It helps the teachers to communicate thousands of students at the same time with the help of different tools of technology. For example, Digital learning becomes one of the significant medium to educate the learner in a very effective manner.
- **To study about the opportunities and changes in the field of education in post-COVID-19 period in India**
    - Technology Driven Education: The current pandemic situation is accelerated of using digital technology which can transform our education system for the better in post-COVID-19 era. The major impact in

education sector in recent years is models with big data tools such as Machine Learning and Artificial Intelligence. These models get to develop their popularity during this pandemic period. These models can be designed to offer personalized teaching based on the learning requirements of a given student which is also helpful for students with special needs, learning disabilities etc. Thus, there is a possibility of habits changing to enable education and it will help in the development of a technology driven era in higher education in India in coming years.

- Collaboration: This pandemic can bring a new opportunity where collaborations can take on a new form among the teachers across the nation to benefit from each other through different online platforms such as webinars, web conferencing, teleconferencing etc.
- Blended Learning: Blended learning is also known as Hybrid learning. This is a combined mixture of synchronous (face to face learning) and asynchronous (online) learning. Thus, in future the educational institutions offering Online-based learning courses can embrace the Hybrid Learning System over the conventional asynchronous systems. However, online-based learning has been able to permeate many layer of our society and the platform is fast becoming an essential tool in transforming the educational system for best. The educational institutions can take up the Hybrid Learning as a tool in their course offerings to get best results in near future also.

- **To study about the long-term impact E-learning in education sector in post-COVID-19 period in India:** E-learning plays a crucial role in educational system and now it has been proved more essential due to current pandemic situation to study from home so that students can resume academics without must gap or not stopped. It can offer a great deal of content, interaction, reinforcement, available in any location and real-time feedback during virtual sessions. Besides, in India different E-learning platforms are getting popular such as Byju app, DIKSHA, Oliveboard, Unacademy, etc. Thus, various E-learning platforms will reach, develop and get better popularity in post-COVID-19 era across all the states in India and it will strengthen and ensure accessibility of learning to all the students. E-learning is helping the students with different information in different ways. Different higher educational institutions have opted for different digital platforms to access learning for their students such as Zoom App, Google Meet etc. However, the educational institutions in India can use present adversity, i.e., digital education as a blessing in this pandemic situation and this will create an opportunity to transform the higher education for better in post-COVID-19 era also.

Suggestions

In the period of crisis, academic institutions should think carefully about their preferences respecting online learning and education technology. Thus, we can mention some suggestions for better improvement:

- There should be well organised department of ICT in every educational Institution.
- Trained teachers should be appointed for operating ICT and training and service condition should also be improved.
- There should be available hardware requirements and software operating knowledge.
- Give stress to provide education through ICT with the help of different tools and techniques.
- Educational institutions need to spend more finance on IT infrastructure in order to get best results in future.

Conclusion

ICT can enable teachers to transform their teaching practices. ICTs are seen as important tools to enable and support the move from traditional 'teaching-centric' teaching styles to more learner-centric methods. ICTs can be used to reinforce existing pedagogical practices as well as to change the way teachers and students interact. It is motivating factor for many students, because it makes education more interesting and joyful. Internet allows students to get additional learning information from that. It makes learning more cooperative, encourages dialogue and creates a more engaging in online classroom. There are many more resources on the internet than the school library, which gives the opportunity to get the information in a highly effective manner. Thus, in conclusion we can say that in post-COVID-19 period, it is expected of using Hybrid Learning System over the conventional asynchronous systems by higher educational institutions to access education. Thus, educational policymakers and administrators can create this crisis as an opportunity to develop new learning models that can reach everyone in higher education level in post-COVID-19 era.

References

Assam Science and Technology Department. (2020). *Use of technology in learning during COVID-19 pandemic.* Retrieved from https://assam.mygov.in/en/group-issue/use-technology-learning-during-covid-19-pandemic/

Chattopadhyay, D. (2020). *COVID-19 and the beginning of the 4th revolution in education.* Retrieved from https://www.abpeducation.com/expert-views/covid-19-and-the-beginning-of-the-4th-revolution-in-education-prof-dhrubajyoti-chattopadhyay-1.1198296

Dornadula, C. (2020). *Post COVID-19 education system.* Retrieved from https://timesofindia.indiatimes.com/blogs/dornadula-c/post-covid-19-education-system/

Gupta, S. (n.d.). *The impact of the coronavirus SARS-CoV-2 on the Education Sector in India.* Retrieved from http://confluence.ias.ac.in/the-impact-of-the-coronavirus-sars-cov-2-on-the-education-sector-in-india/

India Today Web Desk. (2020). *COVID-19: 4 negative impacts and 4 opportunities created for education.* Retrieved from https://www.indiatoday.in/education-today/featurephilia/story/covid-19-4-negative-impacts-and-4-opportunities-created-for-education-1677206-2020-05-12

Lin Ways Team. (2019). *Role of ICT in higher education in the 21st century.* Retrieved from https://stories.linways.in/role-of-ict-in-higher-education-in-the-21st-century-876037c5ff94

Mehta, S. (2020). *Coronavirus: 5 Ways Learning Will Change In Post-Crisis Era.* Retrieved from https://www.entrepreneur.com/article/349285

Oliver, R. (2014). *The role of ICT in higher education for 21st century: ICT as a change agent for education*. Retrieved from https://www. Researchgate.net/publication/228920282

Patrions, H. A. & Shmis, T. (2020) *Can technology help mitigate the impact of COVID-19 on education systems in Europe and Central Asia*. Retrieved from https://blogs.worldbank.org/europeandcentralasia/can-technology-help-mitigate-impact-covid-19-education-systems-europe-and

Srivastava, A. (n.d.). *COVID-19: A Technology Driven Era for Higher Education*. Retrieved from http://confluence.ias.ac.in/post-covid-19-a-technology-driven-era-for-higher-education/

Subarahmanyam, V. & Ravichandran, K. (2013). "Technology & Online Distance Mode of Learning." *International Journal of Humanities and Social Science Invention*, 2(1), 05-13.

World Health Organisation. (2020). *Digital technology for COVID-19 response*. Retrieved from https://www.who.int/news-room/detail/03-04-2020-digital-technology-for-covid-19-response

2
COVID-19 and Its Repercussions on the Cyber Security Landscape

Shan Eugene Palakkal

A Digitally-Connected World

The advent of the novel coronavirus (COVID-19) pandemic has generated massive social and economic changes in people's everyday lives. An invisible foe has swept the globe, catching countries by surprise with its deadly virulence. The COVID-19 pandemic has created uncertainty, anxiety and a drastic change in regard to our way of life. It is a huge humanitarian crisis that has affected global economy too. Traditionally driven by in-person meetings at trade events and markets, the business of content creation, licensing and distribution has been heavily hit by the pandemic-led travel restrictions and thus impacted the work and revenue of content creators/sellers as well as buyers. The disruption of business has left companies struggle their way to maintain security and business continuance. These business have depended on information technology — their data centres, cloud systems, departmental servers etc. have become more vital. However, like all other business activities, technology has been the saviour. The digital infrastructure has skyrocketed.

Due to the COVID-19, just in a single month, the world became far more digitally connected and vulnerable than ever. Companies are using digital channels to pay salaries to the employees, and consumers to avoid hoarding food, medical supplies. Digital health technologies have rapidly expanded and new ways of monitoring healthcare have emerged that have customized in response to the pandemic. Healthcare providers are using chat, phones, email and Telemedicine portals for remote counselling and diagnosis. Various organizations are using digital infrastructure to procure protective supplies for healthcare and hygiene workers as well as to counsel them. Digital channels are providing entertainment for families. People are accessing social media websites like Instagram, Facebook, Twitter etc. more frequently in addition to watching movies by subscribing to web channels like Netflix, Amazon, Hotstar, Zee5 etc. and also indulging in online games by installing various applications. People tend to give permissions to access their personal information readily available on their phones, laptops and social media accounts to use the services provided by the applications. Penetration of Internet is so deep that human life without it seems meaningless.

On 2 April, 2020, the AarogyaSetu app – for pan-India and available in 11 languages – was launched as the main contract tracing technology endorsed by the Central Government. The app got its biggest push when PM Narendra Modi urged the nation to download it while announcing the extension of the national lockdown till May 3. Soon it became one of the most downloaded apps globally, and has crossed the 75 million mark. The app has added on functionalities such as donating to the PM's Citizen Assistance and Relief in Emergency Situations Fund or PM CARES Fund, and hosting e-passes for essential service providers. With no legislation that spells out in details how the online privacy of Indians is to be protected, AarogyaSetu users have little choice but to accept the privacy policy provided by the government. Beyond the legal loopholes, there are technical loopholes as well. The unique digital identity in AarogyaSetu is a static number, which increases the probability of identity breaches. A better approach would be constantly-changing digital identification keys like what Google and Apple deploy in their joint contact tracing technology.

They are also motivating people to make the most of their valuable time in creativity and providing the tools to do so. So also they are helping to shore up our future by enabling children to learn online while schools and colleges are shut. Overall, Internet trends has revealed positive benefits, as people are enjoying the quality of life benefits received in the move to working from home (WFH).

Children are arguably one of the most affected lot during the ongoing second wave of the COVID-19 pandemic. With playdates and excursions out of picture, little ones are forced to spend yet another summer at home this year. But making their summer a tad better now are virtual art and theatre camps. From art and crafts to playwriting and music, summer camps facilitators are coming up with creative exercises to keep children engaged. Storytelling camps give children assurance and positivity in these critical times. Learning crafts and engaging in creative activities keep kids mind off the pandemic.

Companies such as HealthifyMe, Signzy and other techies have created platforms that notify users when vaccine slots open in their districts, eliminating the need to regularly sign in to CoWin with an OTP and Check. Once registered (for free), people receive alerts as soon as a slot opens via SMS, email, WhatsApp and even Telegram. Given the speed at which slots get lapped up in urban areas, the tools offer a better chance of getting appointments. Even if well-intended, the app-based slot booking process coupled with low vaccine availability have made it a 'fastest-finger-first' contest, which is unfortunate. Few people getting instant alerts skews it even ore and that is the issue. Social media is also abuzz with other instances where coders have jumped the queue for shots. Some developers have managed to use coding skills to go beyond just sending alerts and automate the appointment booking process entirely, which could be illegal.

Online lifestyle has been digitally transformed as an exponential change accelerated at home and work via cyberspace. The year 2020 will be remembered as the year that security events exploded and cyber incidents transformed society in different ways.

But the negative cyber security impacts of these changes have led many digital experts to summarise certain events as a growing 'cyber pandemic' too. Hackers and malicious actors have taken advantage of the increased digital wave. From ransomware to data breaches, from election security to unemployment fraud, this biological pandemic has unleashed new challenges. Even the World Health Organisation has seen an increase in the number of cyber attacks directed at its staff, and email scams targeting the public. The bad news is that the cyber landscape is poised to undergo more fundamental changes. Motivations for cyber attacks vary – for (some) nation states, the motivation is geo-political transformation; for cyber criminals, it is increased profits; for terror groups, the motivation remains much the same, but the risk factor may be lower. However, it is 'insider threats' – due to discontent with the management or for personal reasons – that could well become an omnipotent reality.

Cyber Threat Landscape

Lockdowns across the country have forced customers, financial institutions, fraudsters and organized crime alike to be creative, rethinking their operation and adapting to the new reality. Cyberspace has emerged as new playground for espionage. All one requires is a few dedicated hackers who can crawl for information stored on the enemy's servers. Various security organizations should keep an eye out for the emerging threats that are rising.

Several high-profile attacks were reported from the United States. For instance, a major cyber-attack headlined 'SolarWinds' – and believed to have been sponsored from Russia – had rocked the U.S. It involved data breaches across several wings of the U.S. Government, including defence, energy and state. Before the U.S. organizations were hacked in the early 2021 in an unusually aggressive cyber-attack, by a Chinese group Hafnium, which had exploited serious flaws in Microsoft's software, thus gaining remote control over affected systems. Earlier in June 2021, JBS SA, the U.S. subsidiary of a Brazilian meat processing company, was the target of a ransomware attack; the company also paid a ransom in millions. These attacks were all primarily on civilian targets, though each one was of critical importance. Obviously Cyber, which is often referred to as the fifth domain/dimension of warfare, is now largely being employed against civilian targets, bringing the war into our homes.

Zeroing on Healthcare

What is specially worrisome at this time, when a pandemic is raging, is the number of cyber-attacks in health-care systems. With data becoming a vital element in today's world, personal information has become a vital commodity. Compromised 'health information' is proving to be a vital commodity for use by cyber criminals. All indications are that cyber criminals are increasingly targeting a nation's healthcare system and trying to gain access to patients' data. They are becoming more sophisticated, and are now engaging in stealing sensitive data in targeted computers before launching a ransomware attack. Many cyber criminals are known to practice 'reverse engineering' and employ 'penetration testers' to probe high secure networks.

Low hanging fruit, that's how cyber security expert Sandeep Kamble describes the healthcare sector today from the point of view of a cyber criminal. With the number of COVID-19 cases mounting in the past couple of months and hospitals running out of beds, the number of '1800' helplines, government and private tele-medicine facilities and at-home care services have increased expotentially. This also makes users susceptible to cyber attacks. In the past five years, the healthcare industry has featured among the most cyber-attacked industries. Chennai-based Cyber Security Works (CSW) recently analysed 21 top Pharma companies in India and the US that were engaged in COVID-19 research and found that 99 per cent of them had been breached. A few high profile data breaches in India includes Dr. Reddy's and Delhi Medical Council. Personal information of most of the companies were exposed to the dark web, which render them susceptible to impersonation of employees and exposes their critical data. The database links should not be in the public domains, they can be easily hacked. It was found that almost all had open ports, protocols and services which made them ripe for cyber attacks.

The rising popularity of tele-medicine comes with the hazard of more cyber threats. Virtual medical consulting service Myhealthcare, for instance, receives 2000 calls on an average in a day. Tele-consulting service Practo launched services in 15 languages to deal with the burgeoning number of COVID-19 teleconsults. During the second wave, COVID test labs have suddenly mushroomed, where they ask for personal details, documents and online payments to pre-book slots. Unfortunately, most of these labs are fake, but these are desperate times and people don't have the time and energy to distinguish the fake from real. The onus is on digital healthcare providers to get their security in place, but as a user one can create stronger passwords and check the veracity of the account while transferring the money. Apart from identity theft, another cause for concern is the possible breach in the 'internet of medical things'. Medical implants and support devices are connected to the internet to enable location based remote monitoring. This area is gaining momentum especially during pandemic times, when people do not want to visit hospitals. If these devices are exposed to cyber attacks they can malfunction endangering the lives of those wearing them.

Cyber Crimes in Variants

K7 Computing's Cyber Threat Report has found that Kerala recorded the highest number of cyber attacks during 2020. It was found that the threat actors targeted the state with COVID-19 themes attacks aimed at exploiting user trust. The fear and panic caused by the lockdown and rapid spread of the virus has left the public looking for more information on the situation. These actors exploit this fear to their advantage and scam used into downloading malicious software and divulging sensitive information like banking codes. One of the reasons for the high number of data breaches is that India with booming startups and powerhouses is a highly attractive market for Cyber criminals. So also Indian companies are financially well off, they have a brand to deal with apart from the massive amount of personal, financial and user behavioral data that they have.

Social networking plays a major role in cyberspace. Social networking has become so popular among the youth that it might one day replace physical networking. It has evolved as a great medium to connect with millions of people with similar interests. If you use the Internet for online banking, social networking or other services, you may risk a theft to your personal information (if revealed) such as name, address, credit card number etc. Unscruplous people can access information through unsecured connections or by planting software and then use personal details for their benefit. Needless to say, this may land you in trouble. Virus programs are a headache and may get activated if you click a harmless link. Disadvantages outweigh the advantages more because of the security and dangers that is embedded within.

Several types of cyber crimes are hacking, spam, credit card fraud, cyber bullying, phone phreaking, cyber terrorism, software piracy, digital forgery, cyber squatting, child pornography, data diddling, web jacking, cyber stalking, identity theft, denial-of-service attacks, computer worms and viruses and physical damage to the computer etc.

AarogyaSetu app uses both Bluetooth and GPS reference points, which could be seen as an overkill. The app is something of a black box. There is no documentation publicly available on the app. The advocacy groups argue that there should be more transparency on the inner workings of an app that is being promoted by the government and which is asking for the personal details of millions of citizens.

Cyber terrorism is a pre-mediated use of disruptive activities or the threat thereof, in cyberspace, with the intention to further social, ideological, religious, political or similar objectives or to intimidate any person in furtherance of such objectives. It is a negative and harmful use of IT for producing destructive and harmful effects to property, whether tangible or intangible of others. Cyber terrorists use encryption programmed and digital signatures to co-ordinate using email service which cannot be read by anyone.

Pandemic has seen dating apps, where people come looking for love and adventure, and has increasingly become a playground of fraudsters. It all looks like fun, games and a dash of romance to start with. But dating apps have become a minefield with fraudsters using the popularity of these platforms to dupe people. The traffic on these apps has risen by 20-30 per cent in the last couple of months. Earlier this year, several senior corporate executives in Gurgaon fell victim to racketeers who befriended them on a dating app and duped them. If one divulges too much details like address or bank information, salary information in their on dating apps, one can run the risk of falling prey to fraudsters. On 'OKCupid', there has been a 30 per cent increase in messages sent each day globally. Another app 'Bumble' claimed that their overall data indicates a trend of increased use by new and existing users. Some of the cases are not even reported.

Pandemic has created disastrous ripples in the world and all aspects of human life have been jeopardized. Classroom teaching was one of the first and foremost casuality for very obvious reasons as it involves mass gatherings. Given the continuous nature of the teaching-learning process, the administrative mechanism resorted to the only possible solution, that of online teaching and learning, for primary as well as higher education. Online teaching has its merits as it enables learning without boundaries and must be strengthened to complement the educational infrastructure. Respect to all the dedicated teachers who are changing the world with their honest efforts. While children missed school, as much for the fun and games as for the lessons and peer learning, they quickly adapted to contactless learning. Technology has spread its wings in nearly every aspect of School@Home. To begin with, online learning is more personalized than physical learning. For e.g. students can pause, rewind, and repeat lessons which is especially helpful for students with different learning needs. Students can also alter their learning environment, select language options, review their lessons, take a quiz to see how they are faring, get their homework checked and scores delivered faster and discuss doubts with their teachers. If done the right way, online education can be as effective and productive as physical schools.

Phishing, Vishing and other forms of financial fraud have been perpetrated on gullible people for years now. Phishing is use of stolen personal information like customer IDs, iPINs and credit/debit card details by sending emails that appear to be from a legitimate source. Vishing is fraudsters trying to seek personal information like customer IDs, net banking passwords, ATM card details, etc. through phone calls. But with lockdown and restricted mobility, pushing people online, with little provision for security, scamsters seem to have discovered a whole swathe of the population that they can now target. In Madurai (Tamil Nadu), a housewife received a call from a person claiming to be the customer care executive of reputed brand. Stating that she had won an SUV worth Rs.15 lakh for an online purchase made on Amazon recently, the suspect wanted the details of her PAN card, bank account and Aadhaar card to process the delivery of the vehicle. But she sense foul play and disconnected the call. She would have become a victim of a phishing call, but for her suspicion. However, not everyone is aware of the intricacies of such frauds. It is often the temptation of easy money that people fall victim to. They walk into a web of irresistible offers carefully laid out by fraudsters who want to dupe them. By the time law enforcement agencies get into action, the victims would have lost their hard-earned money. Recovery is a possibility by remote, since cyberspace is a world of its own with few boundaries.

Ever since the pandemic began, many volunteers across the country have complained of stalking after sharing their numbers.

A lot of data breaches and issues in cyber security of late has been happening. Thus an app made in Hyderabad, 'Doosra' (which means second, in Hindi) aims to solve issues by providing users with a secondary phone number and blocking unwanted calls. This is how it works : all the calls one receives to the Doosra number, except those in the 'trusted contacts' list' will be blocked. The caller can send a voicemail. The receiver will get to know the caller's number. So the receiver can call them back using the app's 'intermediate number' so that the other person sees neither the receiver's phone number nor the Doosra number. One can disable the call blocker on the app for a specific time or location. One can share the virtual mobile number with others without compromising their privacy.

It is no surprise that the age-old offence of making calls posing as bank officials and asking for ATM card details continues as people still share their credentials after being lured into fake promises, despite awareness messages from banks and the police. The latest in the series of such scams is a group of suspects making calls claiming to be officials from a leading nationalized bank. Taking the name of PM Narendra Modi, the suspects collects details of the ATM card, with the card verification value (CVV) code, for the transfer of Rs. 4500/- as COVID-19 assistance.

Online gaming sites or apps are the next trend. The Department of Telecommunications alone has the powers to block websites under the Information Technology Act. The Madurai Bench of the Madras High Court, has asked the State government to consider passing suitable legislation to regulate and control online gaming. There have been cases where youngsters killing themselves over debts linked to online gambling. Some states like Assam, Odisha, Nagaland, Telangana and Andhra Pradesh have banned or regulated online games. Notices have been sent to popular movie stars and cricketers who endorsed online games in advertisement.

Cyber-squatting is an act of registering, trafficking in or using a domain name with an intent to profit from the goodwill of a trademark belonging to someone else. Pharming is a cyber attack aimed at redirecting a website's traffic to another bogus website. Cheating by impersonation after hacking social media or email accounts was also attempted during COVID-19 pandemic, with suspects operating from other states sending mails/messages to friends/contacts of the account holders, stating that they were stranded due to the lockdown and urgently require financial help. Even the FB account of few IPS officers, including that of Mr. Aggarwal was also hacked. Dhinesh Pandian, an honorary member of the Nation Cyber Defence Research Centre, said frauds involving OTPs, matrimony sites, EMI transactions, false promises on tax benefits and phishing cases were among the most common cases reported during COVID-19 lockdown.

When social media morphed into a COVID-19 war room in the last few weeks with people trying to crowd-source Oxygen, plasma and life-saving drugs, fraudsters skulking in the digital shadows latched on to pry on people's desperation. The modus operandi is similar to the liquor delivery and fake e-tailer scams operating through social media platforms where fraudsters float their phone numbers in the name of known shops. When people call, they are asked to make an advance payment, online. And that is where the trap lies. Once the payment is made, the scamsters switch off their phones and promptly disappear. COVID-19 scam is the flavour of the month. Uncertainty and distress have forced people to let down their guards. The scams are an outcome of the shortage of infrastructure and official resources. Perhaps if we had more organized ways of collating and verifying information and aid being provided, we could reduce instances of blackmailing or siphoning off money. A rip-off costed a life – Mr. X from Mumbai, who was fleeced off Rs.18000/- by a certain 'Mr.Y', posing as a distributor of a leading pharmaceutical company, calls these scamsters the lowest scum on earth. Mr. X was desperately trying to source six Remdesiver injections for a critically ill friend, and he did not think twice when asked to pay in advance only to find out that he had been cheated. The friend passed away in the next three days.

In the course of the second wave of the pandemic that has brought the country to its knees with a staggering number of infections and daily deaths, there has been a growing concern over how it is affecting children. Over the past several weeks, there have been many instances of children whose parents are hospitalized after been affected by the virus and are helpless and left alone at home with little or no support system around them. And a far more tragic scenario is where children have been orphaned as a result of their parent(s) succumbing to the disease. While social media has been largely helpful in amplifying SOS calls for beds, medicine and oxygen, it has also been a hunting ground for those seeking to profit from vulnerable, orphaned children and illegal posts calling for adoption and seeking financial aid for them. One such viral post said, 'if anyone wishes to adopt a girl, please feel free to contact Priyanka (her number was mentioned in the post). One girl is 3 years old and the other is 6 months old. They have lost their parents recently due to COVID-19. Share as much as possible to help them get a life (sic)'. While many chose to re-share and forward this appeal without checking the facts, there were others who immediately flagged it off as being 'irresponsible and an offence' because appeals and request to adopt children through Watsapp and social media messages make kids vulnerable to child trafficking and illegal adoption. While this fake post was called out in time, there are many such messages doing the rounds, that have sparked a conversation about how we need to be cautious and watchful about spreading information about such sensitive issues, which can put a child's life at risk. India has special stringent laws related to adoption. Do not fall for such traps. Reach out to an NGO or Call 1098 for all issues concerning children of all ages. Reportedly Child Rights Body has been receiving pouring requests for adopting kids amid the pandemic.

Sex workers find innovative ways to stay in business during pandemic. If masks are a must for them and their clients, many are taking to striptease and dancing to keep the business running. But what is bringing in the moolah in the time of virus – and keeping them safe from COVID-19 is 'e-sex', as many sex workers take to their smart phones for sex chats and video sex. Many are even getting trained in this new 'art'. Sex workers are trying new ways, even in cities that do not have a red light area. A small section of sex workers has taken technology route through Zoom, Telegram, Watsapp and Skype and accepting payments via e-wallets. The internet is now the only hope of retaining their regular and possibly finding new ones. However, they complain of hurdles – from stiff competition online with many regular people who have good conversational skills and use innovative video broadcasting methods, staying anonymous and broadcasting themselves for a fee to free porn available online. Saheli Sangh, a Pune-based NGO, has issued SOPs to sex workers in Budhwar Peth.

In the current climate where pandemic conspiracy theories are on the rise and racial injustice is being played out on the world state, it had become a responsibility for Facebook and Twitter to remove posts that promote violence. The problem has been exasperated and amplified in recent times, perhaps as people have been spending a lot of time online during lockdown.

Need for a robust Cyber Security Response System

A string of high-profile cyber-attacks in recent months has exposed vulnerabilities in the critical infrastructure of even advanced nations. This has reinforced the need for improved defences against actual, and potential, cyber-attacks by all countries across continents. The law dealing with cyber terrorism is however, not adequate to meet the precarious intentions of these cyber terrorists and require a rejuvenation in the light and content of the latest developments all-over the world. To penalize the cyber offenders and to prevent cyber crimes, the Government of India has passed its first Cyber law, the Information Technology Act, 2000 which came into effect on 17 October, 2000 and India was the 12th nation at that time to adopt cyber laws. This Act is the only one which provides measures for cybercrimes, their punishment and sufficient remedies.

Most nations have been concentrating till date mainly on erecting cyber defences to protect military and strategic targets, but this will now need to change. Today Zero-day software, no doubt exist, though little is known about them. What is, however evident is that a whole new market currently exists for Zero-day software outside the military domain, and the world must prepare for this eventuality.

The Ransomware attacks are punishable under Section 66E and 66F of the IT Act, 2000. Under Section 43 of the IT Act, hacking is a punishable office with imprisonment under section 66B. The offence of phishing is punishable with 3 years imprisonment and a fine up to Rs. 1 lakh in section 66C of the IT Act. Section 66 and 72 provides punishment for cyber-stalking and online harassment.

Also the IPC, 1986 provides with some punishments and remedies for cyber crimes – Section 419, section 354. And people spreading fake news or information can be arrested under Section 505 of the IPC and Section 54 of the Disaster Management Act, 2005 and can be punished with imprisonment up to 3 years and a fine of Rs. 1 lakh or both.

The problem of Cyber laws in India is that there is not set definition of cyber crimes. Though there are some laws and remedies in IT Act, 2000, there are lot of loopholes. There are no specific inclusions or scams against big companies and hence they are to be treated only under the sections of hacking and online fraud. There are no separate laws enacted for handling cybercrimes against the healthcare sectors too.

Territorial jurisdiction is another issue which is not specifically dealt by any cyber law. Since cyber crimes are computer and internet based crimes, the hacker could be sitting far or maybe from another state or a country across the world and hence determination of jurisdiction is difficult. Preservation of evidence is yet another problem. As most of the evidence and proofs are online and in systems, destruction of evidence is easier.

Some of the existing laws are limited only to the theoretical punishment and not easy to prosecute a cyber criminal due to its anonymity. There are no proper measures to take actions against these online criminals and no strategic measures to find these criminals. There should be a Computer Emergency Response Team to deal with cyber crimes.

In recent weeks, television news channels have shared leaked Watsapp chats of film actors in their coverage of actor Sushant Singh Rajput's passing away. This has led to questions about whether communication over platforms such as Watsapp is secure or not. It prompted Facebook-owned Watsapp to come out with a statement on its use of end-to-end encryption to secure user messages. Since 2016, Watsapp has installed an end-to-end encryption system, which says that it 'ensures only you and the person you're communicating with can read what's sent, and nobody in between, not even watsapp'. Watsapp says it responds to requests from law enforcement agencies 'based on applicable law and policy'.

In Chennai, Commissioner of Police Mahesh Kumar Aggarwal decentralized the cybercrime unit, to the police station level, making it easier for victims to lodge complaints. This emerged as a game changer because the time taken to start the investigation in various cases was reduced to less than 24 hours, enabling the police to stop payments by reaching out to the payment gateways. In the last four months, the cybercrime units received 561 complaints related to various online frauds. Timely intervention of investigators helped in the recovery of Rs.1.14 crore. However, the detection/recovery depends on how soon the complaint was given to the police.

Social media has been a great tool for people in these times. We are all trying to help each other. While it is good to stay updated with the latest news, remember to draw the line where necessary. Constant exposure to overwhelming news can reportedly trigger anxiety, especially when one is already battling with one's own problems. Stay informed but take some time off when necessary. Always run a social media check on the phone number to see if there are other complaints of fraud. Do not get taken in by the use of 'verified'; the person could have just checked that the number exists. Scammers tend to use only text so if the person offering help refuses to speak, that is a 'red flag'.

Schools and educators need to use the right software for education and ensure data privacy. Teachers and students should be trained on cyber security laws and what constitutes harassment or inappropriate behaviour. Parental control on internet and mobile devices of children is necessary. Schools must ensure teachers, volunteers and anyone else with access to children is properly screened and trained as well as enforce a policy for reporting child sexual abuse and handling disclosures from children.

Sending out a message inviting people to adopt a child, when anyone of their parent is deceased, due to COVID-19, this way has legal ramifications. It violates the Central Adoption Resource Authority (CARA) guidelines. Such posts could be a racket and lead children into the hands of anti-social elements. The people who do this should be charged under the child protection Acts like Protection of Children from Sexual Offences (POCSO) and JJ Act (Juvenile Justice) because they are exposing children and playing with their lives.

The challenge of fake news and hate speech requires careful consideration and collaboration between government, academia, publishers, social media platforms and civil rights groups. In the meantime, we as individuals must contribute to tackling the issue.

Building deep technology in cyber is essential. New technologies such as artificial intelligence, machine learning and quantum computing, also present new opportunities. Pressure also needs to be put on officials in the public domain, as also company boards, to carry out regular vulnerability assessments and create necessary awareness of the growing cyber threat.

India needs a Cyber Readiness Index to benchmark security practices in all states and Union territories. To succeed in the post-COVID-19 era, technology providers must rethink their strategies and offerings to accommodate a new security landscape.

References

Rajneesh, (2020). "Cheating in Examination can lead to Internet Slowdown", Chamadia, Anil (Ed.), *Mass Media* (A Communication Research Journal), Delhi, 9.

Prof. Chaubey, R K., (2012). *An Introduction to Cyber Crime and Cyber Law*, Kolkata : Kamala Law House, 138.

The Economic Times, 21 May 2020, p. 3.

The Times of India, 14 March 2021, Friday magazine, p. 2.

The Hindu, 6 December 2020, 2.

The Times of India, Chennai Times, 5 May 2021, p. 1.

The Hindu, 13 October 2020, 6.

The Times of India, Education Times, 28 September 2020, p. 2.

The Times of India, 27 November 2020, p. 10.

The Hindu, 26 April 2020, Sunday, p. 12.

The Times of India, 11 July 2020, p. 10.

The Hindu, 6 May 2021, p. 2.

The Times of India, 6 May 2021, Chennai Times, p. 1.

The Hindu – Metroplus, 20 May 2021, p. 1.

The Times of India, 21 May 2021, p. 6.

The Hindu, 14 June 2021, p. 6.

3

Schools Lock but Classes Unlock: Virtual Learning for School Children during the COVID-19 Pandemic

Rajdeep Dutta **and** ***Joyashri Dey***

Introduction

Today the whole world is experiencing a global academic catastrophe, and it might get even worse if we don't handle it immediately. There have been over 1.6 billion school children and adolescents out of school due to the COVID-19 outbreak since March 28, 2020. Approximately, 80 per cent of the world's students are registered (Saavedra, 2020). The world has been impacted by a severe global imbalance, in which many children attended school but did not acquire the requisite fundamental abilities for long-term success. Additionally, even prior to the crisis, the World Bank's "Learning Poverty" assessment revealed that 53 per cent of children, especially in low- and middle countries, are unable to read and comprehend. Unless we act immediately, the consequences could be significantly more severe (Li & Lalani, 2020; Saavedra, 2020). This is extremely pertinent to those concerned about the crisis's adverse effect on children and young people at the moment. Academic damage has grown, resulting in a significant increase in student absenteeism. Additionally, many nations possess educational structures that are quite discriminatory, and all these results would be most severe for underprivileged children (Adedoyin et al., 2020). Today, the methods used for teaching, distributing knowledge, and spreading content via technology and the internet are crucial (during COVID-19). Since the Indian

Ministry of Education responded to the COVID-19 outbreak with recommendations for online learning for school children during the period and school closures to prevent the outbreak from spreading to school children. The purpose of this section is to argue that, in the event of a COVID-19 pandemic; schools should leverage digital technology to encourage students to develop the locks associated with their school learning, notably school locks and class unlocking (Adarkwah, 2021; Roy, 2020; Martineau, et al., 2020).

Opening school lessons on virtual platforms and closing physical schools was a technique used by the government during the COVID-19 outbreak, which resulted in the development of a substantial, typical online learning service. It is highlighted and addressed how crisis methods used by educational institutions, teaching staff, and students face multiple problems and opportunities, and how online learning is distinct from hurdles and an alternative. The educational paradigm would then progressively incorporate digital methods like this one in times of global emergency. Indeed, the current study aims to gain a deeper understanding of the barriers to and opportunities for digital learning in schools, as well as to make recommendations to school administrators, teachers, and students about virtual school teaching-learning settings.

Method

This study is exploratory in nature. During COVID-19, pay attention to the challenges and opportunities confronting schools, teachers, and students. Assam's Cachar district was chosen as the study universe. The study employed theoretical sampling and the saturation principle. The sample size and saturation met with 32 participants, including school heads, teachers, and parents from eight educational blocks in the Cachar district focuses on school operations and initiatives to improve children's education through virtual learning. These blocks and schools were chosen for a variety of reasons, including accessibility and feasibility.

Table 3.1: Sample Selection and illustration

Purposive Sampling		Randomly Selected Samples		
BEEOs	**Schools**	**School Heads**	**Teachers**	**Parents**
Katigorah	Kayarper LPS	1	2	2
Narsingpur	East Nayagaon LPS	1	3	2
Salchapra	Kathal Bagan LPS	1	2	2
Sonai	A.K. Azad LPS	1	2	1
Silchar	Ghungoorpar LPS	1	3	2
Udarband	Parimalbala LPS	1	2	3
Total		**6**	**14**	**12**
Total Participants			**32**	

This qualitative study focused on the evaluation of secondary sources and interviews with participants who had recorded their interactions on mobile phones. The number of participants was determined based on saturation. A study used an unstructured interview for data gathering, whether face-to-face or over the phone. Based on the findings from the study, data collection and analysis happen concurrently. To this end, the interviews, informal discussions, field notes gathered, and then the following rounds of presenting different types of narrative and thematic discussions help to convey an understanding of the issue.

Findings and Discussion

In the following parts, the study discusses the themes of school locks and classes unlocked via virtual learning during COVID-19, as well as the challenges and opportunities for schools, teachers, and students seeking access to education.

School Lock and Classes Unlock: Education during COVID-19

In recent years, the COVID-19 outbreak and the lockdown it triggered have led to adaptations to working and studying from home. The availability of e-learning emerged before the outbreak, but the effectiveness of the phenomenon has gained a new dimension. Although the emergence of digital education as a saviour following the collapse of academic institutions presents numerous obstacles, it also presents various opportunities. Students, teachers, and schools are all intimately bound up with additional issues caused by these online learning initiatives that were rushed and implemented without any thought or care (Xie & Yang, 2020; Zhou et al., 2020). Many times, the adoption of a technology platform can be greatly affected by whether or not it is free. Some of the wide range of technology companies engages in predatory activities to get a footing in the field of education. Because of this, new words have been introduced to the English lexicon, such as "zoom bombing" (Roy, 2020).

In order to fulfil the learning gaps of students during their school shutdown and to unlock their courses, various measures are made by various entities, including students, schools, teachers, and parents, as indicated by the research participants in the study. For example, create a Whatsapp group with parents/guardians (by class), phone numbers of parents/guardians, and a list of local youth volunteers. Study materials, homework, and evaluation via Whatsapp group. Short videos were shared on Whatsapp/YouTube. Local teachers also visited students at their homes. DIKSHA App for accessing and sharing online content with students, Viswa-Vidya Programme 2020 from All India Radio, Silchar, online meetings (Zoom, Webex, Google Meet) with resource people, use of Google Classroom, Google Forms, and mobile calls with students/parents for learning interaction. Some issues and challenges are brought to light in the situation and are repeated and discussed in the interviews and are highlighted in the next segments.

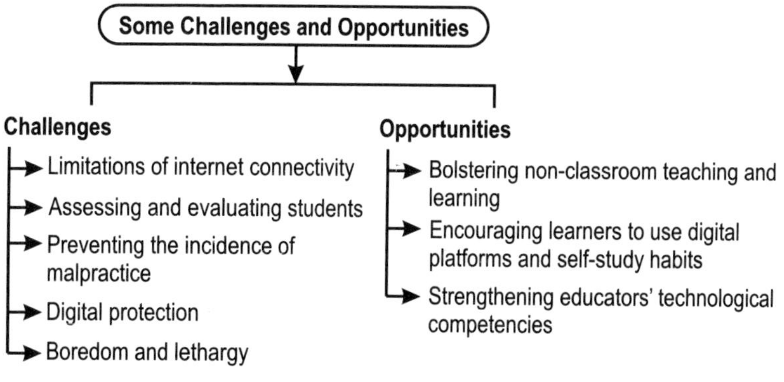

Diagram: Some Challenges and Opportunities.

Challenges

This new outbreak, called COVID-19, has made it evident that the school system is vulnerable to extraneous threats, and many studies rightfully observed that this innovative digital teaching transition was accompanied by a variety of potential problems and behavioural changes. Schools seem unable to conduct their usual educational exercises given the seriousness of the outbreak. To keep classroom instruction on track, the school instructs students to use online learning instead of other learning styles (Dutta & Das, 2021; Lic & Lalani, 2020). However, as indicated by the interviewees, there are several challenges in the planning phase, such as children from different families. It is difficult to generate an online class that suits every learner, failure to produce teaching materials that are highly targeted for independent learning or self-study. Teachers without adequate training cannot effectively integrate new technological tools into teaching, regardless of whether they have or do not have (rich vs. poor). Challenges for the first time, primary-level learners engaged in e-learning in which the learning materials were available online.

- **Limitations of Internet connectivity**

Despite these drawbacks, there is still much to be learned about online education because people who often utilize internet access at home may have insufficient bandwidth or have already spent up their quota. A student shared that,

> *For any meeting, such as a Google meet or Zoom, we student not only find the process of singing in class difficult but logging in itself is frustrating. Getting a broadband upgrade is a simple cure, but it is not always cost-effective or accessible to everyone.*

For such work, the most significant requirement is a tool that reduces the number of steps needed to sign in. We must have an app that enables children and educators to work together and co-create digitally.

- **Assessing and evaluating students**

There is a vital aspect to teaching that consists of evaluating learners appropriately. Due to the school shutdown situation, children are no longer permitted to hold an assessment on the school campus or are required to turn up for an evaluation in their physical setting. According to a head of school,

> *It is possible to evaluate learners in online education using a Multiple Choice Question (MCQ) process as a temporary way of measuring, but evaluating learners based on individual observation is far more accurate — this is one of the most difficult issues for modern e-learning strategies that rely primarily on Multiple Choice Questions.*

Additionally, evaluation is one of the biggest roadblocks for learners. Even if students submit their answer papers online and the instructor is involved in five different sections of instruction, the process of uploading or downloading these entire exam papers is a difficult one. In other words, here, we're talking about a tool that has a reliable monitoring mechanism that simultaneously fulfils the needs of both teaching and learning.

- **Preventing the incidence of malpractice**

There are realities, whether you like it or not, a large number of children who simply exploit the simple path to victory. It has made cheating on a virtual education platform easy for students. When asked, a parent shared that,

> *Children cheat while giving online tests, for example by searching and writing answers from their textbook, at that time they hide themselves from video camera, and also by telling the administrator they were disconnected or have network trouble.*

Furthermore, while it is commendable for schools to emphasize the need for self-discipline, schools should investigate ways to reduce the likelihood that kids may seek to game the evaluation procedures used to improve their own and their peers' learning. To assist instructors in addressing this concern, we have implemented a system-wide feature that notifies instructors when a student exits the testing window to access a webpage or another application. We carefully distribute the questions to ensure that students do not gain an unfair advantage through the use of communication techniques.

- **Digital protection**

Regardless of what activities you undertake online, security and privacy constantly go hand in hand. Typically, educators use free tools, including ZOOM, Google Meet, and Google Classroom, to run their courses on a virtual platform. However, these technologies are not always the safest option or the most secure for educational purposes. One of the most important challenges is to use innovative learning tools that provide a safe education.

- **Boredom and lethargy**

Despite being arguably another major impediment to e-learning, fatigue, and monotony caused by increasing camera time, as well as the practice of remaining in one position for hours, are two significant obstacles. Schools and institutions bear the responsibility for overcoming this dullness or lethargy. Since making engagement as participatory as possible is a priority, and the desire for a continual initiative to uphold that. Therefore, developing the more innovative technologies that are used enable learners to participate in polls or various such exercises that are continue work. Instructors and learners can use a smartboard gadget that provides the opportunity to scribble and sketch on it.

Opportunities

In this situation, e-learning has the chance to thrive because all educational institutions have made the switch to this paradigm. Internet-based learning, working at home, and e-collaborations were extremely popular during the Corona Virus pandemic outbreak. Educational institutions can now seize the opportunity by incorporating an online learning approach into their teaching and learning programmes. Since people have traditionally been comfortable and reluctant to embrace new learning styles, this is going to be an uphill battle. This period of online education will be one when people may see the advantageous effects of e-learning tools. There are ample opportunities to create startling inventions and digital advancements at this moment. When it comes to the use of digital training, both the teachers and the students will be put to the test. It will help pupils improve their real concerns and critical analysis capabilities, as well as their flexibility. No matter what age you are, everyone has the availability of digital educational tools, and this means everyone may have the time and geographical flexibility that goes along with it (Dutta & Das, 2021; Nisanci et al., 2020). Thus, when it comes to technological advancements, the education field has lots of potentials to introduce radical alterations in almost all elements of teaching, training, evaluation, assessment, outcomes, certificates, and degree programmes. There is the additional benefit of stimulating e-learning competition in the market, opening the door for start-up companies to bring digital innovation to the educational field.

- **Bolstering non-classroom teaching and learning**

When the prolonged school shutdown beginning in March 2020 wreaked havoc on the academic calendar, they also stated that while teaching and learning may continue through online learning, specifically via mobile technology, in the absence of learners' physical proximity to institutions, these digital means may encounter certain hurdles that must be given due attention. A teacher drew attention to the fact that,

> *In order to provide high-quality digital learning, I've observed that it poses unique obstacles and has an impact on several parts of academic achievement, along with the interaction between students and teachers, which is essential for learners' progress. The gap created by this technology may not be able to be filled.*

The consensus among several school administrators and educators seems to be that in-class learning is vital, but this needs to be put into context and fine-tuned to present conditions. Studies need to be conducted to plan for the return of learners to the institution. Additional thought must be given to the complexity of complying with physical distance criteria in the school environment due to student figures and classroom sizes. Many institutions have lowered class sizes or separated students from each other in classrooms, but others have found alternative solutions, such as conducting school programmes or providing activities at community locations, like outside of the campus.

- **Encouraging learners to use digital platforms and self-study habits**

In this context, it may be said that several families have faced significant hurdles when it comes to utilizing new technologies and that many parents have encountered obstacles to their skills and the affordability of technology to help their children. Distance education was faced with the difficulty of self-directed study during the outbreak, bringing it to the spotlight. For students, having parents who can assist with their homework and make use of modern technologies like computers, smartphones, and the internet is a given. Thus, their process of learning has to shift when their schools are closed. A student stated,

> *Thanks to a wide range of digital learning platforms – telephone, radio, television, email, and video calls – I have been likely to progress my study and keep social connections with my school, friends, and teachers during the school shutdown periods.*

- **Strengthening educators' technological competencies**

Because virtual learning has relied heavily on technological resources such as email, online classes, Whatsapp, Google Classroom and Pdf document-sharing, YouTube videos making platforms, the issue has highlighted the need for educators to improve their e-learning skills. As the use of digital technologies is a vital component of the professional abilities demanded of instructors to produce effective e-learning content. It follows that several learners are unable to work freely with technology. In addition, teachers have had to prepare learners for new technology while simultaneously using those same devices to conduct lessons.

Recommendations

Following an analysis of challenges associated with schools, teachers, and students' schoolwork, based on the participants' real experiences in the interviews, we have concluded that the following recommendations should be put into effect:

- Increased learning opportunities, with varying levels of adaptation, lead to great technology and teaching working more intimately together.

- The virtual learning platform, together with teaching-learning and other additional materials, as well as workbook-based study notes, is being reconstructed or reformed.
- Concerns about the effectiveness and efficacy of online education. By incorporating graphics, motion, and photographs into online instruction, learners' experience less boredom and fatigue.
- The curriculum must be revised, teaching methods must be enhanced, and online programmes must be diversified. Additionally, the need to develop new criteria for teaching, learning, assessment of students, and quality management has been urged.
- The use of cutting-edge teaching management technology ensures that management is taught and allows schools to be located anywhere in the world without interfering with students' learning.
- Schools in the 21st century should recruit a "lead teacher, teaching assistants, and technological personnel". Educational technology is also used to teach students how to learn on safe and secure digital platforms.
- Encourage home and school education integration while promoting teacher-student and parent-child interactions.

Conclusion

During this unforeseeable catastrophe, learners were able to study via digital platforms due to the availability of virtual education. Nevertheless, the process of online education mirrors some of the issues highlighted previously. Several queries develop new standards and expectations for digital learning including the following: (a) How can schools improve their integration of technology and education?; (b) How do learners learn more via self-study online?; (c) How can educators make online instruction more effective and realistic?; (d) How can parents be guided in dealing with their children's education? Therefore, extensive studies on virtual or digital education are required to handle these issues. With the COVID-19 outbreak serving as a wake-up call, we now know both the obstacles and the benefits of education. Following up on ideas set forth by education professionals as well as potential curriculum guidelines and learning settings could lead to an education roadmap that could be followed once children have returned to school. Additionally, the shutdown of schools for weeks or months has focused attention on the training needs of both pupils and teachers. Teachers must improve their ability to use technology effectively, as students must learn to work more independently. Since the recent trauma has raised the concern that children's psycho-social conditions must be improved, it is critical to foster a positive school, teacher, student, and parent relationship. This supports children's adjustment and ability to adapt following traumatic experiences. Thus, teachers informed citizens, and like-minded people should step up and be advocates for students, with the hope of their participation in education reform and in closing the gaps produced by the COVID-19 pandemic.

References

Adarkwah, M.A. (2021). A Strategic Approach to Onsite Learning in the Era of SARS-Cov-2. *SN Computer Science*, 2 (4), 1-15. https://doi.org/10.1007/s42979-021-00664-y

Adedoyin, O.B., & Soykan, E. (2020). COVID-19 pandemic and online learning: the challenges and opportunities. *Interactive Learning Environments*, 1-11. https://doi.org/10.1080/10494820.2020.1813180

Dutta, R., & Das, B.R. (2021). Social workers' perspectives on children's education during the COVID-19 pandemic: A lesson for India's pandemic second-waves. *International Journal of Applied Research*, 7 (6S), 21-24. https://doi.org/10.22271/allresearch.2021.v7.i6Sa.8605

Li, C., & Lalani, F. (2020). *The COVID-19 pandemic has changed education forever. This is how.* World Economic Forum. https://www.weforum.org/agenda/2020/04/coronavirus-education-global-covid19-online-digital-learning/

Martineau, M.D., Charland, P., Arvisais, O., & Vinuesa, V. (2020). *Education and COVID-19: challenges and opportunities.* Canada: United Nations Educational, Scientific and Cultural Organization. https://en.ccunesco.ca/idealab/education-and-covid-19-challenges-and-opportunities

Nisanci, A., Kahraman, R., Alcelik, Y., & Kiris, U. (2020). Working with refugees during COVID-19: Social worker voices from Turkey. *International Social Work, 63*(5), 685-690. https://doi.org/10.1177/0020872820940032

Roy, D. (November 5, 2020). *5 problems you can face in online learning and how to deal with them.* New Delhi: India Today. https://www.indiatoday.in/

education-today/featurephilia/story/5-problems-you-can-face-in-online-learning-and-how-to-deal-with-them-1738361-2020-11-05

Saavedra, J. (2020). *Educational challenges and opportunities of the Coronavirus (COVID-19) pandemic.* World Bank Organization. https://blogs.worldbank.org/education/educational-challenges-and-opportunities-covid-19-pandemic

Xie, Z., & Yang, J. (2020). Autonomous Learning of Elementary Students at Home During the COVID-19 Epidemic: A Case Study of the Second Elementary School in Daxie, Ningbo, Zhejiang Province, China. *Best Evidence in Chinese Education,* 4(2), 535–541. https://doi.org/10.15354/bece.20.rp009

Zhou, L., Wu, S., Zhou, M., & Li, F. (2020). Best Evid Chin Edu. *'School's Out, But Class On, The Largest Online Education in the World Today: Taking China's Practical Exploration During The COVID-19 Epidemic Prevention and Control As an Example,* 4 (2), 502-519. https://doi.org/10.15352/bece.20.or023

SECTION-II

COVID-19 AND HEALTH

4
COVID-19 and Its Impact on the Mental Health of the Elderly

Bijoy Das

Introduction

Elderly remain very valued and considered as very respectful members in our families and communities. This stage is very sensitive for them as they feel they are a kind of burden and that pushes them into the category of more vulnerable. Generally, they have very little immunity power, poor health status, economic dependence and many times isolated in the family that develop a negative perception for them and have significant psycho-social impact on them. Along with the growing population incidences, the number of elderly is increasing on a rapid scale. WHO (2018) stated that the proportion of elderly population will nearly double from 12.0 per cent to 22.0 per cent from 2015 to 2050. Further it says by 2050 around 80.0 per cent of the older population will be living in low and middle income countries. Currently, there are around 125 million people aged 80 years older and by 2050 that number may increase around 434 million.

The outbreak of COVID-19 also led them at higher risk of more serious complications to the disease. This pandemic of COVID-19 is affecting the life of elderly in a greater way. It has changed their lifestyles in accessing their need and care and support that they require during such pandemic. This group needs special care and support from their friends, family members and communities especially for mental and emotional support and well-being. This pandemic situation made them more vulnerable and resulted in them facing trouble like anxiety, stress and insomnia in their daily lives. An observation from European region found most of the countries affected by this pandemic are elderly (Kluge, 2020). Besides, the concept of social distance in respect to the COVID-19 is badly affecting the mindset of the elderly because they need regular health check-ups, frequent visits by family members and relatives that keeps them strong in social relationships.

Today, there are number of issues related to elderly that are visible in social media, television and in other forms of media. Knowing these issues may cause psychosocial harm to elderly and that is dehumanizing behaviour to them as stated by Kornfeld-Matte (2020). In this century elderly are similarly familiar with social networking sites hence they also get access to information about what is happening in the world. Thus, it affects their mental health status directly and indirectly. As we know mental health is an important ailment in the entire sphere of our life including the older age group. This period remains a great evidence of rise in morbidity, mortality, loss of function related to a common mental disorder. Thus, the present chapter tries to explore the possible mental health challenges those were faced by elderly in this outbreak of COVID-19. Further, secondary sources have been used to collect relevant information and for necessary justification.

Objective of the Study

The present review study is intended to understand the impact of COVID-19 on the mental health condition of elderly population.

Methodology

It is a review article based on the available literature and evidences on elderly and their mental health during COVID. The current research paper is based on secondary data, after reviewing various research papers and articles chronologically. Articles with no mention of elderly and their mental health have been excluded. Selected articles and research papers have been discussed and divided into categories accordingly to meet the aforementioned objective of the study.

Findings

Ageing and Mental Health

Older people have always been facing serious challenges related to mental health. The problems that they are facing during the period of elderly as homelessness, loneliness, economic dependency, physical and emotional abuse—all have a serious impact on their physical as well as mental health. There is great evidence in the rise of morbidity, mortality, hospitality, hospitalization and loss of functional status are related to some common mental disorders among the elderly (Parkar, 2015). As world is rapidly increasing with the number of elderly population that has a direct increase in the age related diseases such as poor mental health, dementia, depression, anxiety, suicide etc. (Parkar, 2015). Other problems like loss of parental rights in older age, negligence and forms of various disasters and global public health issues are similarly responsible for rising mental health issues among elderly. Today, the impact of modernization and the youth oriented society produces a very negative attitude towards the ageing and elderly. In addition Parkar (2015) also stated that of all those factors and witnessed various surveys it is shown that depression is the most common mental disorder in later life. As the context of the study is on the mental health status of the elderly during COVID-19, we will further analyze and discuss various mental health challenges that are being faced by elderly during such an outbreak.

COVID-19 and Mental Health of Elderly

What factors make elderly more vulnerable during this COVID situation? What more do we need to do to deal with the issues of elderly during this outbreak? How COVID-19 has a greater impact on the mental health of the elderly. Well, this pandemic has given a global threat to the world and resulted in it having affected almost all segments of society including the elderly. If we see the global death rate from the beginning of the pandemic – it has directly affected the age group that reflects 15.0 per cent of the first wave deaths in China were aged above 60 years (Banarjee, 2020). In addition, as per Chinese Centre for Disease Control and Prevention stated mortality rate of COVID-19 is in the age group of 60 to 65 years of age (Banarjee, 2020). With all these increasing trends and raising death tolls significantly affecting the mental status of elderly with the fear of loss of lives.

It is very well known to us that factors like psychological, social and emotional are fully associated with aging or elderly. They have severe chances of risk of infections and decrease in all forms of immune system (Banarjee, 2020) thus, the COVID-19 catches those having less immune system categorically it is observed mostly among the elderly. Lie and colleagues (2020) also stated that progression of illness and risk of death is three times higher among the elderly (Cited in Banerjee, 2020). Along with the other issues this pandemic has significant impact such as health issues, anxiety, distress, pain, depression, adjusted disorder, insomnia, etc. and these are mostly relevant to the elderly issues. The protocol of this pandemic stresses on social distancing, isolation those keeps misbalancing the lifestyles of the elderly people. When they need social and emotional support from the other members of family and community, the matter of social distancing causes of loneliness, institutional care such as elderly homes and partially at home. These are causes for risk factors for depression, anxiety, disorders and suicide (Banarjee, 2020). Bhatia and Sud (2020) further agreed to the fact that social isolation is mostly connected to the development of mental health related issues such as depression and anxiety. They further recommended that to prevent mental health issues of elderly, the effects of social isolation must be monitored. Apart from that few studies have also shown that adults 60 and older who have pre-existing medical conditions such as heart disease, lung disease, diabetic or cancer are more likely to have severe, even deadly (Arbaje, 2020).

It is true that social connectedness plays a vital role in promoting mental support during such public health issues especially in ageism. Another factor that can have a significant effect is the highly exposed and excess of information by the media on the death toll triggered by raising anxiety, low mood and disturbances. The fear of getting infected among this group is due to the poor immunity and having general fever and cough during this period. Thus, Bhatia and Sud (2020) similarly mentioned that a less robust immune system is putting them at greater risk. Further, it is also witnessed that feelings of loneliness and being isolated resulted in higher risk factors for poor mental and physical health.

Concluding Discussion

We must assure that we should not leave them behind in our response to COVID-19 whether it is during COVID or Post-COVID situations. They must be treated with respect and dignity (Kluge, 2020) and morally with maintaining all the necessary protocols of social distance (physical distance) and precautionary measures. All communities and stakeholders must be supported to promote necessary interventions for the well-being of elderly people. Professionals like social workers should promote more counselling services for the elderly to maintain a balanced life between their physical and mental health. We should identify and implement the best measures to alleviate stress and anxiety among the elderly during this pandemic of COVID-19. Besides, health and other professionals should also identify the effective medium to reach out to them with the minimum information so that stress and anxiety can be diverted in the means of spirituality, prayer, *yoga* and meditation.

In addition to supporting and strengthening their mental health status Arbaje (2020) suggested practicing physical distance is important rather than social isolation. Arbaje further says that physical distancing doesn't mean isolation or loneliness. Therefore, keeping them safe is important by maintaining physical distance as social isolation can have a negative impact on their immunity and mental health (Arbaje, 2020). There is also a need to take some extra efforts to bring more mental stability among them. They need more space in the family, spending quality time with other members in the family is important and can reduce anxiety and stress during such a pandemic. Hence, Joshi (2020) also suggested promoting emotional well-being, revisiting memories is also important such as watching old pictures, letters, and videos so that these methods help to keep them engaged themselves during this pandemic situation.

Some of Specific Measures

- Help them in handling mobile technologies (cellular phone) using recent apps to make video calls so that they can feel an attachment with other family members or relatives.
- Encourage your friends and family members who stay outside to make regular contact with the elderly parents.

- Keep them away to hear growing death tolls because this has a serious impact on their mental health status.
- Involving elderly people for cooking favourite dishes to enjoy with the other members.
- Find your space to have a quality time with them to support them mentally.
- Keep them busy with playing songs, movies, religious TV serials so that they can develop feelings of attachment in the family.
- Involve them in regular meditation and *yoga* and prayers as some of the spiritual activities to get them to relax from stress.

Future Prospects

- Wide range of studies required to understand the impact of COVID-19 on India's senior citizens.
- Individual can play various roles for promoting the value of social distancing by not hurting the emotions of the elderly.
- Studies require to find out best practices to reduce their mental illness; anxiety, stress and depression.

References

Banarjee, D. (2020). The Impact of COVID-19 Pandemic on Elderly mental health. *International Journal of Geriatric Psychiatry, 35*(12), 1466-1467. Retrieved from https://onlinelibrary.wiley.com/doi/10.1002/gps.5320 DOI: http://doi.org/10.1002/gps.5320

Bhatia, A. & Sud, R. (2020). Why it is important to tend to the mental health of the elderly during COVID-19. Retrieved from https://www.deccanherald.com/opinion/why-it-s-important-to-tend-to-the-mental-health-of-the-elderly-during-covid-19-852770.html

Joshi, M. (2020). Taking care of Elderly at Home during COVID-19. Retrieved from http://www.asl-ap

Liu, Z. (2020). Novel Coronavirus Pneumonia Emergency Response to Epidemiology. The Epidemiological Characteristics of an outbreak of 2019 novel coronavirus disease in China. *Xing Being Xue Za Zhi, 42* (1), 145.

Parkar, S.R. (2015). Elderly Mental Health: Needs. *Mem Sam Monographs, 13*(1), 41-49. Doi:10.4103/0973-1229.153311.

WHO. (2020). Leaders Speaks out about their concerns regarding older people in the context of COVID-19. Retrieved from https://www.who.int/news-room/feature-stories/detail/leaders-speak-out-older-people-covid-19

WHO. (2018). Ageing and Health. Retrieved from https://www.who.int/news-room/fact-sheets/detail/ageing-and-health

Philip, J. & Cherian, V. (2020). Impact of COVID-19 on Mental Health of the Elderly. *International Journal of Community Medicine and Public Health,* 7(6), 2435-2436. Doi.http://dx.org.doi.org/10.18203/12394-6040.ijcmch20202513

5
COVID-19 and Its Impact on Mental Health: A Review

Kshetrimayum Dayananda Singh

Introduction

The origin of the Corona Virus Disease 2019 (COVID-19) pandemic can be traced to Wuhan, China, where the first case of the disease was reported. In India, Kerala became the first state to report a confirmed case of COVID-19 on 30 January, 2020. Subsequently, it spread nationwide and then onto half a dozen other countries between December 2019 and early 2020 (Qin et al., 2020). The rapid spread of COVID -19 pandemic and the threat posed by the deadly disease to the very existence of humankind has led to the adoption of strict measures to contain the deadly virus in the countries across the globe. In an unprecedented scale, imposition of lockdown, social distancing norms, avoiding face to face teaching and learning and restrictions on immigration becomes a common feature in the lives of the people (Kapasia et al., 2020). In this backdrop, one aspect that merits detailed discussion is the impact on mental health of people across different age groups.

One characteristic that is widely noticed among many people in the wake of COVID-19 pandemic is the fear psychosis among general population created by the deadly disease. Islam et al. (2020) conducted a study on what are the factors that led to stress during the COVID-19 pandemic in Bangladesh, it was found that fear of COVID-19 infection (i.e. self/family members) as the one leading factor for causing mental stress among people. In the same study, the possibility of hampering study plan and future career and financial difficulties like loss of income due to proponged lockdown in the wake of COVID-19 pandemic as the main cause of stress like depression, anxiety, phobia, insomnia, etc.

Another important finding in a study carried out by Shoib et al. (2020) underscores the role played by rampant and uncontrolled circulation of an excessive amount of fake news, rumours, misinformation and disinformation on social media, misinterpretation of fever as COVID-19, separation from loved ones and shortage of household commodities and medicines due to lockdown alongside the fear of infection as significant factor affecting the mental health of people during the pandemic.

The seriousness of mental stress caused by the threat of COVID-19 infection can be gauged by the analysis of the 69 Indian suicide cases during the COVID-19 outbreak shows that factors like fear or anticipation of COVID-19 infection were the most prominent suicide causality although most of the victims were later diagnosed with COVID-19 negative as being reported in the press media (Dsouza et al., 2020).

In the light of the above studies, it assumes significance to have a deeper understanding of the wide spectrum of issues related to mental health in the wake of COVID-19 pandemic.

Impact of COVID-19 on Mental Health

The COVID-19 pandemic has fuelled mental stress on a wide range of people belonging to different age groups as there is a sea change witnessed since the outbreak of the pandemic in terms of economic activities, education, entertainment, sports activities, social norms, mobility and interaction of people, both young and old, in a societal setting.

Youth and Children

The paradigm shift from the Pre-COVID-19 interactive environment in the educational setting at all level viz. Primary, Secondary and Tertiary level to online educational system and thus avoiding physical classes and intreactions inside and outside classrooms in the educational institutions in the aftermath of ensuing lockdown has brought in mental stress in the lives of many students. A new problem associated with the adoption of online classroom teaching is that of putting students of poor families and residing in remote or rural areas into difficulties in accessing the online classroom facilites thereby causing mental stress.

UNESCO (2020), has reported that around 320 million learners are affected in India, of which about 34 million belongs to the tertiary level of education. Children are being deprived of the joy and happiness of life. They have been kept isolated from their playmates who are always minding meeting friends and playing with them happily at school. In a recent survey conducted by the Save the Children, an NGO, in which over 6000 children and parents were interviewed in the US, Germany, Finland and the UK, it was found that 65 per cent of the children struggled with boredom and feeling of isolation (Editorial, *The Sangai Express*, 30 July, 2020). School routines gave respite to young people with mental health issues by serving as an effective coping mechanism. When school are close, they lose a substantial degree of fun, curiosity and learning elements in life and their symptoms could relapse (Lee, 2020).

College and university students have been experiencing stress, loss of appetite and sleep problems because of delays in university exam and concern about their future career (Lee, 2020). Due to the closing of schools, colleges and universities, many students are spending 8 to 12 hours a day on the mobile phone for the last four months (Editorial, *The Sangai Express*, August 8, 2020). Young adults are more active on social media (WhatsApp, Facebook) and social networking sites compared to others. They are more prone to be victims of infodemic and this could be the reason for the suffering of mental distress (Shoib et al., 2020).

University Grants Commission (UGC) and the State's Higher Education Department instructed to the academic institution to continue the teaching-learning process through digital platforms so that the students are kept in constant touch with their studies and books (Kapasia et al., 2020). However, the online learning process is at times discriminatory as students from remote areas and marginalized sections find themselves at disadvantaged position while availing online learning facilities due to the lack of electricity, poor internet connectivity and cannot afford a smartphone/ laptop. A recently viral story of a poor father from a rural area of Himachal sold his cow, the only means of his income for the family, to buy a smartphone for his daughter's online class (*NDTV*, 23 July, 2020).

Working Class and Senior Citizen

The working class population has been adversely affected by the new changes that has brought in due to the COVID-19 pandemic. According to a survey by the Center of Monitoring the Indian Economy, 11 per cent of youngsters from 20-24 years of age group had lost their jobs in April 2020 due to nationwide lockdown. The composition of the workforce in India shows a very high share of informal employment. Out of a total of 462 million workers, 422 million were informal workers in 2017-2018 (Dev et al., 2020). The predicaments of informal workers have been compounded by the fallout of the impact of COVID-19 on the working population of the country as the informal workers were already grappling with the problem of low wages and incomes in the pre-COVID-19 period. As of April 2020, there was a loss of 122 million jobs out of that, the small traders and daily wage labourers were 91 million. This lead to thousands of migrant workers from Bihar, UP, West Bengal travelled several thousands of kilometres on foot to reach their native places without any provision of food or shelter in the transit because of lockdown as a fallout of job loss hitting their livelihood hard and thereby causing extreme mental stress and financial insecurity (Choudhari, 2020). Few migrants even lost their lives on the way due to tiredness and lack of food (Dev et al., 2020). Due to the lockdown of COVID-19, a huge number of people are losing jobs in Bangladesh, especially the people of hand to mouth groups. According to Asia Development Bank, about 9 million jobs losses accounting for $ 3 billion GDP lost in Bangladesh during an ongoing lockdown of COVID-19 (Islam et al., 2020).

The agriculture and allied sector in the country was adversely affected by the impact of COVID-19. The farmers have to incur heavy losses due to a lack of buyers and proper marketplace for their agricultural produce. The disruption in the normal supply chain for agriculture and allied sector led to the wastage of vegetables, milk and milk products, etc. It created excess availability of food especially in rural agriculture zones and an acute lack of food in urban zones across the country. On the other hand, many of the farmers more particularly the marginal farmers and tenants faced a huge financial crisis. The money financed by banks in the form of loan became a huge burden as they are not able to repay the loan due to the unavailability of proper marketplace and buyers of their produce due to the impact of lockdown and disruption in the normal supply chain (Tripathi, 2020). The mental stress faced by the farmers in such a situation is immense. The failure to repay the loan could become the contributing factor for some farmers to commit suicide.

Many professionals working in the private sector fall victim to job cuts or salary cuts as an economic consequence of the COVID-19 pandemic. The professionals working in BPOs, malls, manufacturing units, hospitality and entertainments, etc. face lots of hardship due to the slow down in the economy of the country. It may be mentioned that many individuals working in private schools as teachers or supporting staffs across the country faced salary cuts or non-receipt of salary for many months due to the closure of schools.

In the aftermath of the outbreak of the COVID-19 pandemic, the increased financial crisis creates multiple problems like the unavailability of food, medicine, treatment, etc. The economic fallout and occupational deprivation due to lockdown led to individual susceptible to psychiatric issues like depression, anxiety and stress (Dsouza et al., 2020). The maximum effort of the Government to concentrate the health resources and workforce toward fighting COVID-19 has led to a health situation which has, to a certain degree, affected the physical and mental health issues of those old persons who are suffering from chronic illness like Cancer, Cardiovascular diseases and Kidney ailments, etc. that requires continual medical support (Kakunje et al., 2020). In such a scenario, there could create a medical situation in which several people dying from non-COVID-19 ailments could overtake the number of people dying from COVID-19 infection (Bansal, 2020). Moreover, due to the rule of social isolation and lockdown, patients with chronic mental illness had to avoid their routine doctor consultation sometimes.

Health Care Workers

Health Care Workers known as frontline warriors of the COVID-19 pandemics are the highest risk group in this pandemic situation. They are the ones who are placing importance on the call of duty than their health safety and security. Health Care Workers are under immense stress while fighting COVID-19. The contributing factors to their mental stress can be summed up as constant effort on their part to prevent infection, fear of getting infected, long period of quarantine, days of separation from family and loved ones, shortage of personal protective equipment (PPE), long hours work (Kakunje et al., 2020). The unfortunate death of healthcare workers has been rising since the beginning of COVID-19. With the increased exposure of healthcare workers to COVID-19 stigma against them has been on the rise. They are subjected to social isolation and rejection due to their increased contact with COVID-19 cases with the presumption that they may be infected. Violence against doctors also has been reported in certain countries which have added to their misery. All these issues mentioned above has put an enormous strain on the mental health of healthcare workers.

A study on the impact of COVID-19 on the mental health of healthcare workers in China have found that among 1257 participants, they showed that 50.4 per cent had depressive symptoms, 44.6 per cent had anxiety, 71.5 per cent distress and 34 per cent suffered from insomnia. Thus, overall around 70 per cent of healthcare workers who were engaged in COVID-19 duty were reported psychological distress during the pandemic (Lai et al., 2020). Doctor and healthcare workers have shown immense courage to fight against the pandemic. Despite the acute shortage of resources, they have managed to fight the pandemic effectively, so the general populace is duty-bound to encourage them morally and emotionally.

Role of Government to address mental health issues during the pandemic

The Central Government of India along with the State governments has taken up various measures to preserve mental health and boost the morale of all the citizens comprising of different walks of life by activating several interventions like organizing online classes for the students, introducing digital psychiatry consultation, insurance cover for COVID-19 frontline warriors and launched Atmanirbhar Bharat, a package of Rs. 20 lakh crore, to create a self-reliant Indian economy under which various economic measures have been announced for the economic growth of the farmers, migrant workers, cottage industry, middle class and MSME (Micro, Small & Medium Enterprises) sectors.

The following are some of the measures initiated by the Government for effectively tackling the mental stress of the citizens of the country during the COIVD-19 pandemic (Hiremath et al., 2020).

- Information sharing through the website to reduce ambiguity/panic

  The government control COVID-19 website https://www.mygov.in/covid-19; provides all the necessary information related to the pandemic. This includes videos and readable materials on the infection and the necessary measures to be undertaken. This website provides essential real-time information regarding the actual count of cases found to be positive, the number of recovered cases and the number of deaths. This helps citizens to know official information rather than panicking over false information. Various helpline numbers have been shared through the website. The government has launched a central helpline number- 91112397804 for any inquiry about COVID-19. The National Institute of Mental Health and Neuro-Sciences (NIMHANS), Bengaluru launched a toll-free helpline number- 918045110007 for any inquiry about mental health.

- Training and development activities

  The Ministry of Health and Family Welfare, Government of India has provided health advisors, videos, posters and conduct webinars on handling mental health issues of individuals and children during lockdown period.

- Financial measures to reduce strain

  To reduce financial strain, the Reserve Bank of India (RBI) extended three months (i.e. from 1st March 2020 to 31st May 2020) EMI moratorium on repaying of term loans in all respect of term loans in all commercial banks including regional rural banks, small finance banks and local area banks, co-operative banks and all-India Financial Institutions.

Conclusion

The way of life of people across the world has seen a paradigm shift due to the outbreak of the COVID-19 pandemic. Today, people are living in a different world altogether where social distancing, masked face, hand sanitisers and the organizing business through digital platforms are fast becoming not only the normal standard but also the mandatory norms. Though the disease has claimed many lives in our country, the role of the government and the healthcare workers in the fight against COVID-19 and also to bring back the lives of the people to normalcy in terms of economic, health and educational well-being is highly commendable. On the other hand, the dreadful disease has opened a new battlefront impacting the mental health of people of different age groups. It is, indeed, gradually becoming an area of concern for the general populace. The mental issues faced by the youths and children require different remedial measures as compared to the mental issues faced by the working class and senior citizens. Further, same holds true for COVID-19 frontline warriors.

However, certain issues which are central to the fight against COVID-19 need to be emphasized to a much greater degree. The use of face mask, hand sanitisers, use of soaps for individual and frequent hand wash requires regular expenditure from own pocket which cause mental stress for those who are economically very weak. This problem has the potential to pose challenges in the fight against COVID-19. Introduction of a measure that would enable these must use items easily accessible to the economically weak sections of the society will be a welcome step. Another issue that needs to be addressed is the digital inequality faced by some students and migrant workers of rural area. In this regard, the concerned authority's assistance in bridging the digital inequality gap would effectively reduce the mental stress of the students and migrant workers belonging to poor rural families as it will lead to better access to information which will help in making them aware of the relevant knowledge as well as for getting health-related information in time.

References

Banerjee, D. (2020). The COVID-19 outbreak: Crucial role the psychiatrists can play. *Asian Journal of Psychiatry, 50*(2020): 1-2. doi: 10.10/j.ajp.2020.102014

Bansal, S. (2020). Impact of COVID-19 on Operations of Different Sectors. *Extraordinary and plenipotentiary diplomatist*. Retrieved August 14, 2020, from https://diplomatist.com

Choudhari, R. (2020). COVID-19 Pandemic: Mental health challenges of migrant workers of India. *Asian Journal of Psychiatry, 54*(2020): 1-4.doi: 10.1016/j.ajp.2020.102254

Dsouza, D.D., Quadros, S., Hyderabadwwala J. Z., & Mamun, A.M. (2020). Aggregated COVID-19 suicide incidences in India: Fear of COVID-19 infection is the prominent causative factor. *Psychiatry Research, 290*(2020): 1-4.doi: 10. 10161j.psychres.2020.113145

Dev, M.S., & Sengupta, R., (2020). COVID-19: Impact on the Indian Economy. *Indira Gandhi Institute of Development Research, Mumbai Working Paper, 2020-013*, Indira Gandhi Institute of Development Research, Mumbai, India.

Hiremath, P., Kowshik, S.S.C., Manjunath, M., & Sheltar, M. (2020). COVID-19: Impact of lock-down on mental health and tips to overcome. *Asian Journal of Psychiatry, 51*(102088): 1-4.doi: 10.1016/j.heliyon. 2020.e4399

Islam, D.M.S., Doza, B.M., Khan, M.R., & Mamun, A.M. (2020). Exploring COVID-19 outbreak: Crucial role the psychiatrists can play. Asian Journal of Psychiatry, *50*(2020): 1-20.doi: 10.1016/j.ajp.2020.1020888

Kapasia, N., Paul, P., Roy, A., Sha, J., Zaveri, A., Mallick, R., Barman, B., Das, P., & Chouhan, P. (2020). Impact of lockdown on learning status of undergraduate and postgraduate students during COVID-19 pandemic in West Bangal. Elsevier, *116*(2020): 1-5.doi: 10.1016/j.childyouth.2020.105194

Kakune, A., Mithur, R., & Kishor, M. (2020). Emotional well-being, mental health awareness, and prevention of suicide: COVID-19 pandemic and digital psychiatry. Archives of Medicine & Health Sciences, *8*(1): 147-153. doi: 10.4103/amhs.amhs9820

Lee, J. (2020). Mental health effects of school closures during COVID-19. The Lancet Child &Adolescent Health, *4*(6): 147-153. doi: 10.1016/S2352-4642(20)30109-7

Lai, L., Ma, S., Wang, Y., Cai, Z., Hu, J., Wei, N., et al. (2020). Factors associated with mental health outcomes among healthcare workers exposed to coronavirus disease 2019. Jama Network Open, *3*(3): 1-12. doi: 10.1001/jamanetworkopen2020.3976

Nathiya, D., Singh, P., Suman, S., Raj, P., Tomar, B.S. (2020). Mental health problems and impact on youth minds during the COVID-19 outbreak: Cross-sectional (RED-COVID) survey. Social Health and Behaviour, *3*(3): 83-88.doi: 10.4103/SHB.SHB-32-20

Saurabh, K., & Ranjan, S. (2020). Compliance and psychological impact of quarantine in children and adolescents due to COVID-19 pandemic. The Indian Journal of Pediatrics, *87*(7): 532-536. doi: 10.1007/S12098-020-03347-3

Shoib, S., Nagendrappa, S., Grigo, O., Rehman, S., Ransing, R. (2020). Factors associated with COVID-19 outbreak related suicides in India. Asian Journal of Psychiatry, *53*(2020): 1-3. doi: 10.101/j.ap.2020.102223

Sangai Express. (2020, August 4). Impact of COVID-19 on mobile phone users among youths in Manipur, *The Sangai Express.*

Sangai Express. (2020, July 30). Children's psychology and lockdown intervention. *The Sangai Express.*

Tripathi, A. (2020, June 10). Footprints of COVID-19 across the unorganized sector in India. *Ipleaders.* Retrieved August 14, 2020 from www.blog.ipleader.in. https://main.mohfw.gov.in.(last accessed 8th August, 2020)

6

Stress and Emotional Responses of Dakshin Dinajpur in West Bengal as a Result of the COVID-19 Pandemic: A Mixed Method Analysis

Priya Mondal

Introduction

A cluster of pneumonia cases was registered in the Chinese province of Hubei in December 2019 (Lu et al., 2020). The infection was later discovered to be caused by a virus known as SARS-CoV-2. Coronavirus disease 2019 is the name given to the illness caused by this virus (COVID-19). As the COVID-19 pandemic and its far-reaching consequences play out around the world and in our culture, it is natural for people to have a variety of thoughts, emotions, and reactions, including: feel anxious or overwhelmed. Anxiety, worry, or fears are all examples of racing thoughts. Sadness, weeping, and a lack of interest in previously pleasurable practices. Increased heart rate, stomach upset, fatigue, or other unpleasant feelings are examples of physical symptoms. Rage irritability, or frustration, agitation or restlessness, unable to help yourself, sleeping problems or inability to concentrate, feeling cut off from other people, anxiety about going to public places, and difficulty unwinding. In the face of such a big obstacle, all of these emotions are understandable. In our attempts to slow the spread of transmission, there has been the loss of life, rapid changes to our way of life (e.g., research, work, social gatherings), and disrupted plans due to travel restrictions and social (physical) distancing steps. People are naturally worried about their own health and safety, as well as the health and safety of their loved ones. There is also a great deal of confusion. Recognize the gravity of the public health issue confronting our society, and keep in mind that responding from a position of panic and fear is rarely helpful, particularly in the long run. Taking care of our health and well-being at times like these will help us cope with stress and enable us to remain calm and productive in the face of the global crisis.

The purpose of this work is to address the effect of COVID-19 on the mental health of the global population, as well as its causes and consequences. The subjects that have received the most attention in the scientific literature have been included, the majority of which affect not only healthcare practitioners and officials, but the entire population. Furthermore, some steps that could be taken to reduce the pandemic's emotional toll were discussed.

Psychiatric Disorders Caused by the COVID-19 Pandemic

Changes in Habits on a Day-to-Day Basis

Sleep disturbances, a serious disorder linked to anxiety, depression, and suicidal activity, have increased during the SARS-CoV-2 pandemic, according to an analysis of sleep quality (Sher, 2020a). In addition, poor sleep quality increases irritability and, as a result, complicates family cohabitation. Another intriguing research looked into news monitoring: higher averages of time (3h) spent focusing on the virus outbreak were linked to the development of anxiety symptoms (Huang and Zhao, 2020), as well as social responsibility principles and compliance with social distancing guidelines among US adolescents (Huang and Zhao, 2020). (Oosterhoff et al., 2020). Individuals who were evidently vulnerable to "optimism bias", the assumption that they are less likely to develop the disease than others, on the other hand, showed less involvement in risk mitigation behaviours. This concept can also be used in other diseases, such as lung cancer (Soofi et al., 2020).

Highly personalized Stress Response

Individual variations and stress-mediated contexts have a significant impact on emotional reactivity in periods of psychological distress. An analysis of the general population in Italy sought to determine which gender and personality characteristics were more strongly linked to psychological effect during the COVID-19 pandemic (Moccia et al., 2020). Individuals with nervous, cyclothymiacs, and/or depressed temperaments are expected to experience further emotional effect as a consequence of the current situation, according to the findings. Meanwhile, male gender, as well as stable and avoidant adult attachment styles, were found to be protective against the risk of increased psychological distress.

Psychological distress represents several conditions that affect people

During this pandemic, one of the key assessed topics, anxiety, has been dramatically rising in society (Huang and Zhao, 2020; Li et al., 2020; Qiu et al., 2020; Teufel et al., 2020). Before and after the declaration of COVID-19 in China on January 20, 2020, a research group in China studied the online posts of about 18,000 Chinese social media users and discovered a rise in terms that mirror negative emotions such as anxiety, depression, and frustration (Li et al., 2020). One form of anxiety in particular is worth mentioning: health anxiety. The COVID-19 pandemic offers a once-in-a-lifetime opportunity to investigate the psychological effects of a condition that, on the one hand, presents a severe threat of infectious illness, a threat to a person's physical and psychological integrity, and, in the long run, a massive socio-economic impact. It also allows researchers to determine the psychological effect of an unusual administrative decision like "lockdown" on the general public. This is the first study of its kind to look at the psychological effects of the COVID-19 pandemic on the general population. The epidemic has had an impact on the Indian subcontinent for two weeks and is still at its peak.

People who are addicted to Alcohol

Some countries have banned the selling of alcohol during the lockdown. The reasons for keeping the restrictions included diminished capacity of those under the influence of alcohol to enforce prevention measures, the role of alcohol in domestic abuse, the effect on the immune system, and, ultimately, the high cost of acute drinking on emergency services (Nadkarni et al., 2020). Nonetheless, a higher percentage of patients suffering from addiction developed abstinence syndrome as a result (Narasimha et al., 2020). After lockout, twice the amunt of extreme abstinence syndrome (seizures, delirium tremens, and hallucinations) occurred every day in a psychiatry emergency service in Bangalore, India (Narasimha et al., 2020). In addition, India has seen an increase in the black market for alcohol, non-consumable alcohol intake, and even suicide among those suffering from addiction (Nadkarni et al., 2020). Indeed, it has been suggested that alcohol consumption is a significant risk factor for the decompensation of psychological disorders and, as a result, could predispose people to commit suicide, especially those who are fragile and vulnerable (Conejero et al., 2020).

Children

During the pandemic, children, especially the young, are particularly vulnerable. This increases even when they have restricted social connections at home, which are essential for identity and well-being at a young age, as well as decreased physical activity, isolation, and boredom (Fegert et al., 2020; Jiao et al., 2020; Loades et al., 2020), all of which can have long-term consequences (Fegert et al., 2020; Loades et al., 2020). Indeed, mental and physical well-being, as well as adult productivity, are all influenced by the years spent in childhood (Loades et al., 2020; Wang G. et al., 2020). Children who were subjected to exclusion interventions were five times more likely to seek mental health treatment and to develop PTSD, according to data from past epidemics (Loades et al., 2020). It has also been shown that children who are not in school (i.e., weekends and summer vacations) have longer screen times, erratic sleep schedules, and poor diets (Wang G. et al., 2020), all of which can be particularly dangerous over longer periods of time, such as the pandemic's still uncertain length. Furthermore, recent events have triggered the expansion of remote jobs, causing schools and daycare centres to have to halt their operations. As stress levels rise, the family and work environments have fused, resulting in reduced success in both spheres (Mental Health COVID-19, 2020).

Students in College

College students are also vulnerable to drastic changes in their routine and, as a result, to the psychological effects of the pandemic, as colleges have temporarily closed during this global health emergency (Khan et al., 2020). In reality, having a graduation impacted by the pandemic has already been linked to higher rates of depression (Duan L. et al., 2020). Living away from home, a fluctuating family income, and a lack of access to technology to attend online classes are all factors that which aggravate this situation (Cao et al., 2020; Khan et al., 2020). Indeed, the effect of online classes on mental health is a subject that merits further investigation, as it can lead to overburdening (Dubey et al., 2020). A suicide pact involving online classes has been recorded between a private university student and his mother, as an extreme example. Suicides have also been recorded as a result of depression following an exam postponement and the inability to access online classes.

Villages are suffering

Also, some family members returning from the cities are not allowed in West Bengal villages. As the coronavirus disease (COVID-19) spreads across the globe, India faces a new major challenge: how to protect and care for its poor and marginalized citizens living in urban slums. It did, however, make its way into our country, with the first positive case being filed on 17th March, 2020 when the country and the Union Government were embroiled in the CAA controversy. The number of COVID-19 positive cases began to grow steadily in all states, prompting the Union Government to acknowledge the grave threat. When the world began to shut down, people struggled to get back to their homes. When I arrived in my village in West Bengal's Dakshin Dinajpur district, life was normal. Whether it was crop farming or manual labour, people were preoccupied with their respective occupations. The "Janta Curfew" was announced unexpectedly. The farmers were oblivious to what was going on. The local government attempted to raise awareness about the coronavirus, but they were unable to visit every village due to a lack of time. In addition, MLAs were being traded in the state legislature. Farmers are the ones who suffer the most during the lockout. Many of them do not have groceries at home, except for wheat and rice. They are also cash-strapped and unable to afford essentials. The small shops in the village, where they would have been able to get some credit, are all out of stock. Farmers and low-wage workers seldom have enough money or basic needs on hand. They buy in small quantities depending on their immediate needs. The villagers supported each other for a few days, but now everyone is experiencing the same shortage. The elderly are becoming more concerned as their pensions are not being paid on time. As a result, they are unable to get their prescriptions. They are unable to see a doctor or seek treatment in a hospital because doctors are not available in the government facility. The condition for people with disabilities is much worse. Employees who were migrant workers were also in deep trouble. Owing to a shortage of employment and transportation, many of them were forced to walk thousands of kilometers to return home. One of these groups was discovered after walking for four days. We asked them why, as the government had promised, they didn't just stay in one place and get everything they wanted during the lockdown. They clarified that they couldn't stay and they wanted to return to their villages because they had left their children behind. If they are unable to care for the children, they will starve to death. Despite having been screened and promising to spend 14 days in isolation, the party was denied entry to the village after seven days.

Methodology

Respondents and procedure

A cross-sectional online survey of 100 people in West Bengal was conducted between March 24th to May 18th, 2020 for the quantitative analysis. The questionnaires were distributed electronically via the Qualtrics online portal to avoid personal interaction during the outbreak (www.qualtrics.com). The electronic survey link was shared on Facebook and WhatsApp. Participants were asked to read an informed consent form and indicate whether or not they wished to participate in the study before beginning the survey. They were only allowed to answer the questionnaire after giving their consent. Participants had to be at least 18 years old and able to communicate in Hebrew to be considered for the analysis. Being under the age of 18, which is the cut-off age for requesting parental consent; providing answers that followed a similar pattern (e.g. selecting the same answer for several consecutive items or for the entire questionnaire); or failing to complete the entire questionnaire were all exclusion criteria. (Specifically, people who started but did not finish the questionnaire were not included in the study.) The research included participants who completed the entire questionnaire but left out a single demographic question, such as gender or health status.

The qualitative research looked at a random sample of 100 people from West Bengal (50 women and 50 men). Participants were approached via social media advertisements and asked to participate in a research study and a personal phone interview. Many who were interested sent an email to the researcher, who responded by calling them and explaining the report. Those who wanted to participate were contacted by phone for an interview. The consent form was read aloud to the participants before the interview, and they gave their informed consent. Due to the closure and the rules on social distancing, the interviews were performed over the internet.

Traumatic experiences to COVID-19 were evaluated using three questions related to concern, anxiety, and stress triggered by COVID-19, which were focused on previous studies conducted among the general public. "To what degree do you worry about COVID-19?" Participants were asked to react on a five-point Likert scale, with 1 equalling not at all and 5 equalling a lot. A composite index was developed using the averages of all items, with a higher score indicating more negative emotional reactions to COVID-19. The index's internal accuracy was outstanding.

Gender, age, years of education, marital status (married/divorced/widowed/single/other), number of children, medical conditions (yes/no), health status (poor/fair/good), home isolation after the COVID-19 outbreak (yes/no), and services that would make dealing with COVID-19 easier (more details about COVID-19/professional support/lay support/working from home) were among the socio-demographic variables.

Statistical analyses

Descriptive statistics were used to describe participants' demographic characteristics and the research variables.

Qualitative study

Methodologies

Six authors independently gathered data by conducting a thorough and non-systematic search of the PubMed, Cochrane, Scopus, SciELO, and Google Scholar databases. "COVID-19", "SARS-CoV-2", "anxiety", "depression", "psychiatric disorders", "social alienation", "behaviour changes", "psychiatric patients", "mental health", "suicide", "media", "racism", "healthcare workers", "elderly", "domestic violence", "sleep", "LGBT society", "homelessness", "foreigners", "rural community", "informal settlements between March 24th and May 18th, the search was performed. Between the 18th of May and the 8th of September, this article was revised. The authors critically reviewed and selected recent papers, published case series, consensus statements, recommendations, meta-analyses, systematic reviews, and prospective cohort studies for the quest. In addition, research was conducted in the public domains of informative official websites and the references found in the previously collected data.

The respondents' socio-demographic profile

The vast majority of respondents (97.8%) had learned of the COVID-19 pandemic and were familiar with the virus (98.7%). The majority of respondents (95.9%) recognised COVID-19 symptoms, such as fever, cough, shortness of breath, and sneezing; however, none of the respondents recognized myalgia or body aches and pains as a symptom. Nearly three-fifths (77.7%) of those polled listed ways to avoid COVID-19, such as social distance, hand washing, cough etiquette, and mask use. The majority of respondents (96.3%) supported the government's decision to impose a 21-day lockout and (61.9%) were pleased with the actions taken by the federal and state governments to combat the COVID-19 pandemic.

Knowledge and attitude of the respondents towards Corona virus disease 19 pandemic

Majority (99.6%) of the respondents did not come in direct contact with COVID-19 patients, and only a miniscule (4.5%) percentage of respondents had confirmed COVID-19 patients in their locality.

Near about 7 per cent of the respondents were associated with care of suspected or confirmed COVID-19 patients.

Psychological impact of corona virus disease 19 pandemic on the respondents

Near about five-seventh (71.8%) and one-fifth (24.7%) of the respondents felt more worried and depressed, respectively, in the past 2 weeks. Near about one-third (37.1%) of the respondents became more irritable in the past 2 weeks. Half of the respondents (52.1%) were preoccupied with the idea of contracting COVID-19 and one-fifth (21.1%) of the respondents were repeatedly thinking of getting themselves tested for the presence of COVID-19 despite having no symptoms. Minority of the respondents kept checking their fever with thermometer repeatedly (9.7%) and visited doctor (1.6%) on multiple occasions to rule out the symptom of COVID-19 and did routine blood tests (3.4%) to be sure that their health was normal in the past 2 weeks. Near about one-third (33.1%) of the respondents reported of having disturbed sleep-wake cycle in the past 2 weeks. One-fifth (19.9%) of the respondents were taking hydroxychloroquine as a prophylaxis for COVID-19 as advised by the ICMR. A worrying fact was one-tenth (10.8%) of the respondents were taking the drug without any doctor's advice. Majority of the respondents were worried more than usual about their own future as well as future of their family members (57.8%) and worried about the financial loss they were incurring during the period of lockdown (69.6%). One-fourth (25.6%) and one-fifth (34.7%) of the respondents got more depressed and worried, respectively, after reading COVID-19-related news on WhatsApp or Facebook. Majority of the respondents were spending time during lockdown either by doing household chores (62.9%) or working from home (54.8%). Only a minority of the respondents took help of psychiatry helpline (2.2%), started on anti-depressant or anti-anxiety drugs in the past 2 weeks (2%), and was taking sleeping pills (4.5%) for the past 2 weeks. Near about one-tenth (9.1%) of the respondents had thyroid disorders. Majority (64.9%) of the respondents found that COVID-19 pandemic had affected their mental status to some extent. One-fourth (25.6%) and one-third (30.8%) of the respondents found that COVID-19 pandemic had threatened their existence and they found it difficult to adjust to the new routine during 21-day lockdown period, respectively.

Results and Discussion

In the sense that it measured the psychological effect of COVID-19 on the general population in West Bengal, the Index survey is exceptional. After cases began to rise in India in the second week of March 2020, the Central Government issued the first travel advisory, requiring any passenger arriving from abroad to undergo a 14-day self-quarantine. We are on the sixth day of the lockdown time as I write this article. The total number of COVID-19 cases in India and West Bengal is 1356 and 22, respectively. [two] It has already claimed the lives of 46 people across India, including three in West Bengal. The majority of the respondents were male, well educated, living in urban areas, and working in private employment, according to the socio-demographic profile. While this survey made a deliberate effort to exclude healthcare professionals, healthcare providers accounted for nearly one-tenth of the respondents (11.2%).

The majority of those polled were aware of COVID-19's signs as well as the precautions that should be taken to prevent the disease from spreading. This gave the impression that public health awareness campaigns were spreading across society. The majority of respondents agreed with the government's decision to impose a 21-day lockout and praised the measures taken by the federal and state governments to combat the COVID-19 pandemic. This demonstrated that the general public was willing to put their personal agendas aside for the common good.

In the previous two weeks, almost half of the respondents (57%) and one-fifth of the respondents (15%) felt more worried and depressed, respectively. This level of extreme worry and depression is much higher than what we usually see in a population study. In the previous two weeks, almost one-third of the respondents were more irritable. Despite having no symptoms, half of the respondents were preoccupied with the possibility of contracting COVID-19, and one-fifth of the respondents considered getting screened for the presence of COVID-19 on a regular basis. Given the disease's highly infectious nature, this result came as no surprise. In the previous two weeks, nearly one-third of the respondents said their sleep had been disrupted. This was also higher than the group sample's confirmed incidence of non-organic insomnia. According to the ICMR, one-fifth of the respondents were taking hydroxychloroquine as a COVID-19 prophylaxis. One-tenth of the respondents were taking the medication without the recommendation of a doctor, which was concerning. The majority of respondents were more concerned than normal about their own future and the futures of their family members, as well as the financial loss they would suffer during the lockdown. This is unsurprising, given that the condition was previously unknown, and there was every chance that the lockdown would be prolonged as the infection showed no signs of abating. The risk of financial loss weighed heavily on the minds of the majority of the respondents because they worked in private jobs. After reading COVID-19-related news on WhatsApp or Facebook, one-fourth and one-fifth of the respondents became more depressed and concerned, respectively. COVID-19 has been the subject of a lot of negative news over the last two weeks on social media (new cases, deaths, stigmatisation of the cases, lack of personal protective equipment for the healthcare providers, and fake news of new cases in the locality). This instilled in the respondents a sense of doom and gloom.

Despite efforts by the National Institute of Mental Health and Neurosciences in Bengaluru, the Indian Psychiatric Society (IPS), the parent body of Indian Psychiatrists, and the Indian Psychiatric Society, West Bengal State Branch, to assist people in emotional distress during the COVID-19 pandemic through a dedicated helpline, only a minority of respondents (2.2%) used it. Two-thirds of those polled said the COVID-19 pandemic had impacted their mental health in some way. During the 21-day lockdown period, one-fourth and one-third of the respondents, respectively, felt threatened by the COVID-19 pandemic and found it difficult to adapt to the new routine. This is evidence that the current situation has been very stressful in terms of the mental well-being of the respondents in question, necessitating adjustment on their part to get used to a new routine during the lockdown phase.

Conclusion

The COVID-19 pandemic presents a significant medical threat to humanity. Many of us have never seen the steps taken to stop the epidemic from spreading. This pandemic is expected to have a long-term socio-economic effect. The aim of this survey was to get a glimpse into the psychological effects of the pandemic when it was still at its height. Worry and sleep disturbances were widespread among respondents in the previous two weeks, according to the index survey. The pandemic posed a serious threat to the respondents' lives and had a negative impact on their mental health.

References

Rubin, G.J., Wessely, S. (2020). Coronavirus: the psychological effects of quarantining a city. *BMJ Opinion*; 368:m313.

Thakur, V., Jain, A. (2020). COVID 2019-suicides: a global psychological pandemic. *Brain Behavior Immun*; S0889-1591:30643-7.

Liu, X., Kakade, M., Fuller, C.J., Fan, B., Fang, Y., Kong, J., et al. (2012). Depression after exposure to stressful events: lessons learned from the severe acute respiratory syndrome epidemic. *Compr Psychiatry*; 53:15-23.

Maunder, R., Hunter, J., Vincent, L., Bennett, J., Peladeau, N., Leszcz. M., et al. (2003). The immediate psychological and occupational impact of the 2003 SARS outbreak in a teaching hospital. *CMAJ*; 168:1245-51.

Duan, L., Zhu, G. (2020). Psychological interventions for people affected by the COVID-19 epidemic. *Lancet Psychiatry*; 7:300-2.

Sa, L. (2020). How much "Thinking" about COVID-19 is clinically dysfunctional? *Brain Behavior Immun*; S0889-1591:30682-6.

7

Maternal Health Issues, Challenges, and Factors during COVID-19 Situation

Swapan Banerjee and *Pragya Sharma*

Introduction

1. Maternal Health during COVID-19 Outbreak

India had its first reported case of COVID-19 on 30 January, 2020. The issues have been on a gradual rise to date. The initial instances had their history traced back to Wuhan, China, UAE, or Italy. People from these countries were either working or studying there, started returning to their homes for future complications. Directly or indirectly, this is the beginning of COVID-19 in India.[1] Fear of COVID-19 was already widespread by the time initial cases surfaced in India. Many of the expecting mothers seeking a diet chart asked only for a purely vegetarian diet plan citing the fear of COVID-19. The situations were under rumored that infection was due to animal meat, poultry, or seafood. Naturally, meat consumption was going down worldwide until the guidelines came in, clearing the doubts around the spreading of COVID-19 through animal meat.[2, 3]

2. Challenges for Expecting Mothers during COVID-19

There were few critical challenges during COVID situations, mainly lockdown phases for pregnant mothers. All the existing medical government services were almost overburdened, with insufficient COVID tests, transportation problems, improper infrastructures of government facilities and amenities. Even doctors were not available physically at trade but only teleconsultation. Here are some critical points highlighted.[4]

2.1. Nationwide lockdown

There was an announcement made by Honorable PM on the night of 24 March, 2020 for a 21-day extended nationwide lockdown, which was further followed by three more phases of lockdown extending till 31 May, 2020. The lockdown announcement again instilled a sense of fear among the population, and people began hoarding items, including ration, medicine, and other necessary things.[5, 6, 7]

2.2. Psychological Impact

Amidst all this, the fear of an expecting mother was even more as she was carrying a new life with herself. She was facing new challenges everyday, like fear of going for regular anti-natal care (ANC) check-ups as roads were brigaded. There was a fear of an invisible and unknown virus of COVID-19, except the people having an emergency were stepping out.[8, 9]

3. Economic issues

With the announcement of the lockdown, the economy of the nation came to a standstill. According to the guidelines, only essential services, including medical services, fire brigade, Police, ambulance, grocery shops, virtual goods transportation, and similar others, were allowed to function on minimum staff to ensure physical distancing. All private and government offices which didn't fall under essential services were asked to remain shut. Later, some companies/organizations started work even being at home through virtual mode.[12, 13, 14]

4. Migrant labour and other workers

Migrant workers who used to work in metropolitan cities as daily wagers had no other option except to move back to their hometowns and villages. Though the government tried its best to make these people understand their food and shelter with other necessities. There was still a widespread state of anxiety and confusion, and people weren't ready to listen. They started walking when no transport facility was available. Consequently, state governments had to make arrangements for these workers to return home, but it was a matter of time-taking.[15] The population belonging to low socio-economic groups and people employed in informal sectors seemed to be worst affected by the COVID-19. They were daily workers to earn their bread and butter and support the family. This informal sector was concerned with the account for about 93 per cent of the working population, i.e., about 139 million in number.[16, 17]

5. Social aspects

Human is a social being and society plays an essential role in an individual's social, emotional, and mental well-being. Human beings are gregarious animals that always seek social validation and acceptance. This way, the global pandemic came with the guideline of social distancing, which could be exhausting for those who are living in nuclear families. During lockdown phases, they weren't meeting friends and hanging out, which led to frustration and tension that, overall, could not build an actual home environment. This had given rise to some social problems like an increase in the number of suicide cases in the country.[10]

Another major issue was conflict and fights with family members in which often the women were the victims. There has been increasing in the cases of domestic violence that were consequently leading to miscarriages. It was very pathetic that women were always targeted and not spared even in pregnancy. There has been a subsequent surge in the number of domestic violence cases during the lockdown phases compared to the data of the last ten years. India has launched a Whatsapp Helpline number 7217735372, and the national helpline number is 181, while women police helpline numbers are 1091 and 1291 to tackle domestic violence in COVID-19 phases.[11, 18]

6. Health issues and comorbidities

India, as a nation, faces a triple burden of malnutrition, which is undernutrition, overnutrition, and micronutrient deficiencies. All these three forms of malnutrition affect pregnancy outcomes. On the one hand, we have other observations that the mothers are malnourished and enter pregnancy with stunting or thinness (underweight). According to NFHS-4 data, about 11 per cent of women are stunted, and 23 per cent found skinny during pregnancy. On the other hand, we have problems like overweight and obesity, around 21 per cent, according to NFHS-4 data.[19] Issues like gestational diabetes mellitus, pregnancy-induced hypertension, anemia are most prevalent in rural India. Anemia is one of the significant health issues found among 53 per cent of pregnant women, according to NFHS-4 data. Due to the fear of COVID-19, there is a decreased level of exercise, hence fewer physical activities. In general awareness by doctors and nutritionists, pregnant women are advised to walk inside their homes at specific intervals to prevent excess weight and some pregnancy-related complications. However, to tackle these issues at home, expecting mothers can have a diet typical of these issues. Mothers need to be encouraged to take iron-folic acid tablets during pregnancy as the records from NFHS-4 data. It shows an impoverished data of about 30 per cent of women taking I & FA for 100 or more days during pregnancy.[20, 21]

Every second, a woman during pregnancy is suffering from anemia. The consumption of IFA during pregnancy should begin from the second trimester, i.e., the fourth month to 180 days. Apart from that, deworming tablet albendazole (400mg) after the first trimester should be continued (during the 2nd trimester). The mothers can also be encouraged to consume iron-rich food items like *bajra* flour, sprouted pulses, green leafy vegetables, and fruits. Consumption of tea, coffee, and high fiber foods should be discouraged with iron-rich foods for better iron absorption in the body.[22, 23, 24]

Table 7.1: Estimates of Maternal deaths, Worldwide Trend: 2010-2017[25]

UNICEF Region	2010	2011	2012	2013	2014	2015	2016	2017
East Asia and Pacific	27000	27000	26000	25000	24000	23000	22000	21000
Europe and Central Asia	1900	1800	1700	1700	1600	1500	1500	1400
Eastern Europe and Central Asia	1600	1500	1400	1400	1300	1300	1200	1200
Western Europe	330	320	300	290	280	270	270	260
Latin America and Caribbean	9100	8700	8500	8300	8200	8100	7900	7700
Middle East and North Africa	5900	5800	5800	5800	6000	5900	5800	5800
North America	640	660	660	670	680	730	770	760
South Asia	**86000**	**80000**	**75000**	**71000**	**67000**	**63000**	**60000**	**57000**

Sub-Saharan Africa	212000	210000	208000	207000	206000	203000	202000	200000
Eastern and Southern Africa	82000	80000	77000	75000	74000	72000	71000	70000
West and Central Africa	130000	130000	131000	131000	132000	131000	131000	131000
Least developed countries	151000	147000	144000	141000	139000	136000	133000	130000
World	**343000**	**334000**	**326000**	**319000**	**313000**	**306000**	**300000**	**295000**

In Table 7.1, we have just complied with the data in a single table from 2010 to 2017 as available data in UNICEF and WHO to estimate maternal mortality ratio (MMR; maternal deaths per 1,00,000 live births) 2010-2017. The highlighted bold part in the middle of the table is the South Asia area, where all the eight countries are grouped (Table 7.2).[25-27]

Table 7.2: Estimates of Maternal deaths in India and neighbour countries, 2010-2017[25]

UNICEF Region	2010	2011	2012	2013	2014	2015	2016	2017
Afghanistan	11000	11000	10000	9600	9300	8400	8100	7700
Bangladesh	8100	7700	7300	6900	6500	6000	5500	5100
Bhutan	33	31	30	29	28	26	25	24
India	**55000**	**50000**	**47000**	**44000**	**41000**	**38000**	**37000**	**35000**
Maldives	67	62	60	58	56	54	54	53
Nepal	1900	1700	1600	1400	1300	1400	1100	1100
Pakistan	10000	9900	9600	9400	9200	9000	8400	8300
Sri Lanka	140	130	130	130	130	120	120	120

In this review study, apart from shortlisting and computation, we have also analyzed the data available from the websites.[25-27] The analyzed data based on maternal mortality from 2010 to 2017 as available on the respective websites is secondary data. The countries considered in total, i.e., 183, where India is highlighted to find out the status till 2017. In the year, 2010, the rate was highest as per the mean value observed. Further, it is being observed that the maternal morbidity rate (MMR; maternal deaths per 1,00,000 live births) is in reducing state gradually from 2010 to 2017.

As per analysis and available current data, despite the rate decreasing form, the world still has to work hard to make all the necessary arrangements for the mothers until the rate is satisfactory.[28, 29]

Table 7.3: One-Sample Statistics based on 8 years analysis of Maternal deaths (N=183 countries, worldwide)[25]

Year	Mean	Std. Deviation	Std. Error Mean
Average	92.00	52.972	3.916
2010	**1881.70**	**6696.811**	**495.043**
2011	1822.31	6501.347	480.593
2012	1782.66	6408.894	473.759
2013	1741.13	6267.675	463.320
2014	1711.33	6152.630	454.815
2015	1666.57	6022.904	445.226
2016	1642.75	6036.594	446.238
2017	1610.04	5953.742	440.113

Table 7.4: One-Sample Test - based on 8 years of analysis of Maternal deaths Sig. (2-tailed) 0.000; N=183 countries, worldwide[26,27]

Total 8 Years 2010-2017	t	Mean Difference	95% Confidence Interval of the Difference	
			Lower	Upper
Average	23.495	92.000	84.27	99.73
2010	3.801	1881.705	904.94	2858.47
2011	3.792	1822.306	874.05	2770.56
2012	3.763	1782.656	847.89	2717.42
2013	3.758	1741.131	826.96	2655.30
2014	3.763	1711.328	813.94	2608.72
2015	3.743	1666.574	788.11	2545.04
2016	3.681	1642.754	762.29	2523.22
2017	3.658	1610.044	741.66	2478.42

7. Improper medical services and complications

During pregnancy, the mother's immune system focuses on not producing any anti-fetal immune response. This might result in the mother's comparatively weak immune system to make things easier for the growing fetus.[30, 31] In the situations, hospitals are overburdened and are concentrated on treating and managing COVID-19 patients; hence the maternal and child care departments are seriously affected. According to UNICEF, India will be witnessing the highest number of childbirth during this pandemic, with almost 20.1 million expected births. This might come as bad news for many mothers as there won't be enough healthcare force available for them due to this pandemic situation.[22, 23] There would be a high chance of declining medical supplies due to disruption in transportation. The conditions are going to be affecting the women who are under the low socio-economic strata of society. In general, these mothers are dependent on getting their IFA tablets and micronutrient-rich snacks from ASHAs or Anganwadi's under the ICDS scheme.[32, 33, 34]

8. Advice and Suggestions

The mothers are the most critical parts of society as well as a country like India. Despite several issues, non-governmental organizations, academicians can take the initiative and the government and its policy to strengthen the mother's health and nutrition. In the COVID pandemic, mothers from rural India and the lower middle class also take the pain to combat the situations due to scarcity of doctors and other medical facilities at governmental costs.[35] Childbirth and total nutrition are essential to concern during and post lockdown diet and basic calorie measured food. Immunity is often low in poor people due to a lack of protein and vitamins in the mother's body in the so-called areas. So they need a high protein diet in a planned way with the consultation for or counselling with a doctor or gynaecologist and dietician. They can help with the health and nutrition part to progress as best as possible, even at low or affordable costs.[36, 37]

8.1. Maternal Health Manageable at Home

Pregnancy is a normal phase of life through which almost every woman goes and gets a precious life. It has been observing that ancient wisdom and the simple act of eating right and eating safely are indigenous cultures in India for hundreds of years. However, now in current times, stepping out from home can be risky for any individual, keeping in mind the daily cases of COVID-19. As per various sources, India is making records everyday because of approximately 60,000 to 70,000 cases daily. Therefore, managing maternal health at home becomes vital just based on doctors' advice and sometimes dieticians. An appropriate diet and considerable physical activity should be there for a pregnant mother for a good pregnancy outcome, not in India but worldwide.[38, 39]

8.2. Labour Pains and Role of Family and Society

Family and society play a significant role during pregnancy, while the situation becomes more critical in these unprecedented times during the COVID-19 pandemic. A lively and cheerful environment at home is conducive to a good pregnancy outcome, while guidance from elders in the community must be helpful. Grandmothers, sometimes hired nurses or nannies, are taking a vital role in anti-natal and post-natal total care while government or private medical services are not sufficiently available. In a nutshell, a stressful environment and violence at home can lead to many pregnancy-related complications and lead to an unfavourable pregnancy outcome. It is also noticed that women in nuclear families have a good relationship with their husbands and other family members. They get better medical assistance, antenatal care, and have institutional deliveries. At the same time, women living in joint families might have better check-ups and medical help if they have good relationships with in-laws.[40, 41]

Social support is also critical in getting a good pregnancy outcome. Social support is considered an aid received from society, which may comprise neighbours, friends, and community members in need. It is observed that those who have some social support have a lower level of stress throughout their pregnancy, irrespective of their age, trimester, and socio-economic background. The husband has a critical role to play during the pregnancy phase. He should have patience and be empathetic towards his wife. He should ask her about medications, micronutrient supplements, etc. The husband must avoid smoking when she is around to prevent the lady from passive smoking, leading to complications during pregnancy. The total caring attitude of him on her health status is highly desired. Her husband's consultation should be noted following the reporting to Gynaecologist/family physician.[44, 45]

During the COVID phases, many countries have restricted their hospitals from allowing pregnant ladies to bring any delivery coach. As per emergency rules, the spouse or any other family member to the hospital avoid the unnecessary crowd at the hospital. Some data shows that in some families, grandparents or respective guardians are less interested in admitting to maternity wards of government hospitals or sub-standard nursing homes to deliver their child; instead, they prefer home delivery. The reasons may be lack of transport, financial, infection-risks, reliability, or other reasons. Home-based deliveries could result in complications for both mother and child as there are not enough experienced to face the emergency as qualified midwives or birth attendants.[42, 43, 46]

8.3. Psychological Stress of Mother

During the phase of pregnancy, a woman may have a lot going on in her mind related to this whole new experience of childbearing. This might lead to severe liver disorders, stress, and anxiety, resulting in problems ranging from poor health.[47] The improper functioning of all systems in the mother's body may affect the child's low brain development. Hence, total physical and psychological development may also be hampered. The constant stress-cum-anxiety may also lead to severe issues like ADHD and ASD and increase socio-emotional problems in the child *vice versa*. The stress among mothers may also occur in miscarriage, low birth weight (LBW) babies, preterm babies. Babies born from such mothers almost having a chance by undergoing stress and anxiety in the coming days.[46-48]

The factors are well-linked to behavioural, social, and mental health issues. Several factors should be noted concerning dealing with stress and anxiety issues among mothers. These include physical activity, social inclusion, and social support. These factors can be helpful to a great extent in dealing with mental health issues among expecting mothers. They should be aware that physical distancing is the need of the hour and not 'social distancing.' They should be encouraged to talk to their near and dear ones and do whatever makes them happy. They can take up a hobby to get diverted from stress. *Yoga, pranayam* can also help to correct mood.[46-48]

8.4. Post-natal Care and Breastfeeding

After childbirth, breastfeeding should be initiated within an hour. If in case of cesarean birth or any other reason, it is not possible to breastfeed within an hour, breastfeeding should be initiated as soon as possible by the mother.

There is no substantial evidence of the risk of vertical transfer of COVID-19 to date. Even if the mother is tested positive, the child should not be separated from the mother.

The mother's necessary measures like using masks, face shields, and proper handwashing for about 40 seconds before breastfeeding the child. If the mother doesn't want to breastfeed the child directly or has severe symptoms of COVID-19, she can also opt for expressing milk if she wants the child to get her milk. The expressed milk should be fed to the child by a healthy staff member in clean utensils, and the pump used for expressing milk should be washed thoroughly as per the doctor/trained nurse or manufacturer's instructions written on the label on the bottle.[49, 50]

8.5. Immunity during Pregnancy

During the phase of pregnancy, the immune system of the pregnant mother is suppressed. It acts differently when compared with the immune system of a pregnant woman to protect the growing fetus. The fetus has paternal genes that are different in composition than that of the mother's body. Hence, the fetus could be recognized as a foreign entity. In studies, it is found that the fetus is instead considered as an allograft to let grow inside the mother's womb. During pregnancy, there is a decrease in the lymphocyte count of the expecting mother. COVID-19 also causes a reduction in the number of lymphocytes. These monocytes and neutrophiles are the primary phagocytes of the body.

These monocytes and neutrophiles are the primary phagocytes of the body. The rise in phagocytes helps in protection and quick recovery from infection.[54-58] There are several immune-boosting foods available, which can probably lower the risk of mortality by increasing immunity. More than the physiological, it is the psychological impact[59, 60] of phagocytes that help protect and quick recovery from infection.[51-54] There are several immune-boosting foods available, which can probably lower the risk of mortality by increasing immunity. More than the physiological, it is the psychological impact.[61, 62]

Pregnant and lactating mothers are often ignored and not provided total health and nutrition care in developing countries like India. Usually, societies are male-dominated for centuries in India, where women in rural areas are exploited and considered as unnecessary burdens for the families. Low-income family members are not also aware of adequately due to socio-economic reasons. From childhood, a baby girl to an adult mother remains uneducated. During the lockdown and unlocking phases of the COVID-19 pandemic, these maternal issues and total healthcare were found much more crucial due to improper infrastructures and overburdened medical facilities.[63-65]

Conclusion

Maternal health, particularly in the eastern and north-eastern regions, has focused on their mental, social, and psychological challenges. Further, all the maternal issues, challenges, and factors are discussed with some fundamental analysis. Most importantly, the best possible immunity-boosting diet plan that is maintainable at home to cope with pre- and post-lockdown phases among middle-class pregnant and lactating mothers is also emphasized. It is expected by 2030, India would be one of the best countries having significantly little maternal mortality rate (MMR) just because of awareness on mothers' total health and nutrition.

Notes

1. Cucinotta, D., & Vanelli, M. (2020). "WHO declares COVID-19 a pandemic." *Acta Biomedica, 91*(1), 157–160. https://doi.org/10.23750/abm.v91i1.9397
2. "India's first coronavirus infection confirmed in Kerala." https://www.thehindu.com/news/national/indias-first-coronavirus-infection-confirmed-in-kerala/article30691004.ece. Accessed on 25 September, 2020.
3. "Coronavirus very likely of animal origin, no sign of lab manipulation: WHO" https://www.cnbctv18.com/healthcare/ccoronavirus-very-likely-of-animal-origin-no-sign-of-lab-manipulation-who-5746241.htm . Published on 21 April, 2020. Accessed on 25 September, 2020.
4. "Birth in the time of COVID-19." www.statnews.com. Accessed on 25 September, 2020.
5. Dubey, S., Biswas, P., Ghosh, R. et al. "Psychosocial impact of COVID-19." *Diabetes Metab Syndr*. 2020;14 (5):779-788. doi:10.1016/j.dsx.2020.05.035
6. "India will be under complete lockdown starting midnight—By Narendra Modı." https://economictimes.indiatimes.com/news/politics-and-nation/india-will-be-under-complete-lockdown-starting-midnight-narendra-modi/articleshow/74796908.crom=mdr. Accessed on 25 September, 2020.

7. The Lancet. (2020). "India under COVID-19 lockdown." *The Lancet, 395*(10233), 1315. https://doi.org/10.1016/S0140-6736(20)30938-7.
8. "COVID-19 pandemic and challenges for socio-economic issues, healthcare and National Health Programs in India" (2020). *Diabetes & Metabolic Syndrome: Clinical Research & Reviews.14* (5). 757-759.
9. Emergency, P.H., Concern, I., & Health, M. (2020). *Mental health and psychosocial considerations during the COVID-19 outbreak.* March, 1-6.
10. "Lockdown rise of domestic violence, how to tackle situation." *National Commission for Women.* www.indianexpress.com/. Accessed on 25 September, 2020.
11. Krishnan, T., Hassan, S., Satyanarayana, V., & Chandra, P. (2020). "Domestic violence during the COVID-19 pandemic: Lessons to be learned." *Indian Journal of Social Psychiatry, 36*(5), 120-125. https://doi.org/10.4103/ijsp.ijsp_264_20.
12. "Opinion: Impact of COVID-19 on the Indian economy." https://government.economictimes.indiatimes.com/news/economy/opinion-impact-of-covid-19-on-the-indian-economy. Published on 7 April, 2020. Accessed on 27 September, 2020.
13. Banerjee, S. (2020). "Role of Food Companies to Supply Nutritious Foods as per Buyers' Changing Lifestyles, Buying Habits and the Recent Trends." *International Journal of Innovative Research in Science, Engineering and Technology, 9*(3), 1062-1067.
14. Verbeke, Wim. (2005). "Consumer acceptance of functional foods: socio-demographic, cognitive, and attitudinal determinants." *Food Quality and Preference, 16*(1), 45-57.
15. "District Level Household & Facility Survey, NFHS-4 Report." www.rchiips.org. Accessed on 27 September, 2020.
16. "Coronavirus in India: Desperate migrant workers trapped in lockdown." Published on 21 April, 2020. https://www.bbc.com/news/world-asia-india-52360757. Accessed on 27 September, 2020.
17. "Migration in India and the impact of the lockdown on migrants." Published on 10 June, 2020. https://www.prsindia.org/theprsblog/migration-india-and-impact-lockdown-migrants. Accessed on 28 September, 2020.
18. Banerjee, S., & Samaddar, B. (2020). Similarities and celebrations of culture between Bengal and Bangladesh during the COVID-19 phases. Unpublished article. Accessed on 27 September, 2020.
19. NFHS-4 Report. www.rchiips.org. Accessed on 27 September, 2020.
20. "Operational Guidelines." www.anemiamuktbharat.info/.Accessed on 27 September, 2020.
21. Shivalli, S., Srivastava, R.K., Singh, G.P. (2015). "Trials of Improved Practices (TIPs) to Enhance the Dietary and Iron-Folate Intake during

Pregnancy—A Quasi-Experimental Study among Rural Pregnant Women of Varanasi, India." *PLOS ONE, 10*(9): e0137735.

22. "Why pregnant women face special risks during COVID-19." Published on August 2020. https://www.sciencemag.org/news/2020/08/why-pregnant-women-face-special-risks-covid-19. Accessed on 27 September, 2020.
23. "Pregnant mothers and babies born during COVID-19 pandemic." https://www.unicef.org/. Accessed on 27 September, 2020.
24. Banerjee, S. (2020). "Implementation of the vegan diet among obese hypothyroid housewives living in metro cities—A review." *International Research Journal of Medical Sciences, 8*(1), 21-24.
25. "Estimates of Maternal deaths, Trend: 2000-2017." http://mmr2017.srhr.org/. WHO, UNICEF, UNFPA, World Bank Group, and UNPD (MMEIG) September 2019. Accessed on 28 September, 2020.
26. "Maternal health & mortality data." https://data.unicef.org/. Accessed on 28 September, 2020.
27. "Factsheets, maternal mortality." https://www.who.int/. Accessed on 28 September, 2020.
28. "Maternal mortality: Level and Trends.2000-2017." www.mmr2017.srhr.org/ . Accessed on 28 September, 2020.
29. Nohara, M., Miyagi, S. (2009). "Family support and quality of life of pregnant women during pregnancy and after birth." *Nihon Koshu Eisei Zasshi. 56*(12) 849-862.
30. Naja, F. and Hamadeh, R. (2020). "Nutrition amid the COVID-19 pandemic: a multi-level framework for action." *Eur J Clin Nutr*. https://doi.org/10.1038/s41430-020-0634-3.
31. Rico-Mesa, J.S., White, A., & Anderson, A.S. (2020). "Outcomes in Patients with COVID-19 Infection Taking ACEI/ARB." *Current cardiology reports*, 22(5), 31.
32. "Boosting immunity is the need of the hour." https://www.thehindu.com/news/cities/chennai/boosting-immunity-is-need-of-the-hour/article31212288.ece/. Published on 30 March. Accessed on 27 September, 2020.
33. "Ayurveda's immunity-boosting measures for self-care during COVID-19 crisis." Ministry of Ayush, Government of India. Accessed on 2 June, 2020.
34. Banerjee, S. (2020). "Role of Food Companies to Supply Nutritious Foods as per Buyers' Changing Lifestyles, Buying Habits and the Recent Trends." *International Journal of Innovative Research in Science, Engineering and Technology, 9*(3), 1062-1067.
35. "COVID-19 guidelines. Central Council for Research in Ayurvedic Science." Ministry of AYUSH, GoI, 2019, New Delhi. http://www.ccras.nic.in. Accessed on 27 September, 2020.

36. Banerjee, S., Srivastava, S., & Giri, A.K. (2020). "Possible nutritional approach to cope up COVID-19 in Indian perspective." *Advance Research Journal of Medical and Clinical Science, 06*(06), 207-219.
37. Allendorf, K. (2010), "The Quality of Family Relationships and Use of Maternal Healthcare Services in India." *Studies in Family Planning,* 41: 263-276.
38. Banerjee, S. (2020). "Uses of technologies & social media for diet and exercise awareness among obese, hypothyroid, and pre-diabetic women – A case study in West Bengal." *Journal of Xi'an University of Architecture & Technology, 12*(3), 4682-4688.
39. Banerjee, S., & Samaddar, B. (2020). "Impact of COVID-19 Lockdown on Overweight Typically Managed by Easy Diet Planning—A Mini-Review." *International Journal of Technology, 10*(1), 19-22.
40. Faramarzi, M., & Pasha, H. (2015). "The role of social support in the prediction of stress during pregnancy." *Journal of Babol University of Medical Sciences, 17*(11), 53-60. https://doi.org/10.22088/jbums.17.11.52
41. Thapa, S.B., Mainali, A., Schwank, S.E. and Acharya, G. (2020), "Maternal mental health in the time of the COVID-19 pandemic." *Acta Obstet Gynecol Scand,* 99: 817-818.
42. Lewis, S., Lee, A., & Simkhada, P. (2015). "The role of husbands in maternal health and safe childbirth in rural Nepal: a qualitative study." *BMC Pregnancy and Childbirth, 15*(1), 162. https://doi.org/10.1186/s12884-015-0599-8.
43. Britta C. Mullany, S. Becker, M.J. Hindin. (2007). "The impact of including husbands in antenatal health education services on maternal health practices in urban Nepal: results from a randomized controlled trial", *Health Education Research, 22* (2).166-176.
44. Das, B.K., Fatema, U.K., Hossain, M.S., Rahman, R., Akbar, M.A. (2014). "Analgesic and anti-inflammatory activities of the fruit extract of Ampelocissus latifolia (Roxb) on laboratory animals." *British Journal of Pharmaceutical Research.* 4(12):1477-1485.
45. Barakat, E.M.F., El Wakeel L.M., Hagag, R.S. (2013). "Effects of Nigella sativa on the outcome of hepatitis C in Egypt." *World Journal of Gastroenterology; 19*(16):2529-2536.
46. Emergency, P.H., Concern, I., & Health, M. (2020). "Mental health and psychosocial considerations during the COVID-19 outbreak." *World Health Organization,* March, 1-6. Accessed on 27 September, 2020.
47. Banerjee, S. (2018). "A Study on Relationship between Hypothyroidism and Non-Alcoholic Fatty Liver Disease among Obese Women in Kolkata Intervening with Diet." *International Journal of Research and Development, 3*(10), 43-48.

48. Heidi Preis, Brittain Mahaffey, Marci Lobel. (2020). "Psychometric properties of the Pandemic-Related Pregnancy Stress Scale (PREPS)." *Journal of Psychosomatic Obstetrics & Gynecology, 41*:3, pp. 191-197.
49. Lowe, B. and Bopp, B. (2020), "COVID-19 vaginal delivery–A case report." *Aust N Z J Obstet Gynaecol, 60*: 465-466. doi:10.1111/ajo.13173.
50. Milne, S.J., Corbett, G.A., Hehir, M.P., Lindow, S.W., Mohan, S., Reagu, S., Farrell, T., & O'Connell, M.P. (2020). "Effects of isolation on mood and relationships in pregnant women during the COVID-19 pandemic." *European Journal of Obstetrics, Gynecology, and Reproductive Biology, 252*, 610-611. https://doi.org/10.1016/j.ejogrb.2020.06.009
51. Sridama, V., Pacini, F., Yang, S.-L., Moawad, A., Reilly, M., & DeGroot, L.J. (1982). "Decreased Levels of Helper T Cells." *New England Journal of Medicine, 307*(6), 352-356. https://doi.org/10.1056/NEJM198208053070606.
52. Naja, F., and Hamadeh, R. (2020). "Nutrition amid the COVID-19 pandemic: a multi-level framework for action." *Eur J Clin Nutr*. https://doi.org/10.1038/s41430-020-0634-3.
53. Rico-Mesa, J.S., White, A., & Anderson, A.S. (2020). "Outcomes in Patients with COVID-19 Infection Taking ACEI/ARB." *Current cardiology reports, 22*(5), 31.
54. Bogoch, II., Watts, A., Thomas-Bachli, A., Huber, C., Kraemer, M.U., and Khan, K. (2020). "Pneumonia of unknown etiology in Wuhan, China: potential for international spread via commercial air travel." *J. Travel Med.* 272: 1-3.
55. Zhu, N., Zhang, D., Wang, W., Li, X., Yang, B., Song, J., Zhao, X., Huang, B., Shi, W., Lu, R., Niu, P., Zhan, F., Ma, X., Wang, D., Xu, W., Wu, G., Gao, G.F., and Tan, W. (2020). "A novel coronavirus from patients with pneumonia in China, 2019." *N Engl J Med*. 382: 727-33.
56. Emergency, P.H., Concern, I., & Health, M. (2020). "Mental health and psychosocial considerations during the COVID-19 outbreak." *World Health Organization*, March, 1-6. Accessed on 27 September, 2020.
57. COVID-19 pandemic—impact on food and agriculture. http://www.fao.org/2019-ncov/q-and-a/impact-on-food-and-agriculture/en. Accessed on 27 September, 2020.
58. Reissman, D.B, Watson, P.J., Klomp, R.W, Tanielian, T.L, and Prior, S.D. (2006). "Pandemic influenza preparedness: adaptive responses to an evolving challenge." *J Homel Sec Emerg Manag*. 3, 1-24.
59. Dalton, L., Rapa, E., Stein, A. (2020). "Protecting the psychological health of children through effective communication about COVID-19." *The Lancet Child and Adolescent Health*. 4: 346-347.
60. Cobb, T.D. (2001). *Reclaiming our food: how the grassroots food movement is changing the way we eat*. Storey Publishing, Adams, MA, USA. https://

www.amazon.com/Reclaiming-Our-Food-Grassroots-Movement/dp/1603427996.

61. Hislop, T.G., Bajdik, C.D., Balneaves, L.G., Holmes, A., Chan, S., Wu, E., et al. (2006). "Physical and emotional health effects and social consequences after participation in a low-fat, high-carbohydrate dietary trial for more than 5 years." *J Clin Oncol*. *24*: 2311-7.
62. Gleeson, M., Nieman, D.C., and Pedersen, B.K. (2004). "Exercise, nutrition, and immune function." *J Sports Sci*. 22: 115-25.
63. Duerr, H.P., Brockmann, S.O., Piechotowski, I., Schwehm, M., and Eichner, M. (2007). "Influenza pandemic intervention planning using InfluSim: pharmaceutical and non-pharmaceutical interventions." *BMC Infect Dis*. 7: 76.
64. Valdés-Ramos, R., Martínez-Carrillo, B.E., Aranda-González, I.I., Guadarrama, A.L., Pardo-Morales, R.V., Tlatempa, P., et al. (2010). "Diet, exercise and gut mucosal immunity." *Proc Nutr Soc*. 69: 644-50.

8
Teacher Well-being and Stress Management during COVID-19

Gadigeppa M. Sunagar

Introduction

Education as a proximate means progress of society. Thus, one of the aims of education is to bring about desirable changes in the learner in respect of knowledge, skills and attitudes, in such a way, that one may effectively perform the changing roles in a changing society. Therefore, education has been regarded a matter of Primary national importance, and an indispensable agency in the difficult task of building a nation.

Sharma (2010) states that teachers are the pillars of the society, who help students to grow to shoulder the responsibility of taking their nation ahead of others. They desire security, recognition, new experience and independence. When these needs are not fulfilled they become tense. Dissatisfaction among workers is undesirable and dangerous in any profession; it is suicidal if it occurs in teaching profession. If factors responsible for dissatisfaction can be differentiated, attempts can be made either to change those conditions or to reduce their intensity so as to increase the holding power of the profession.

As educators, a high level of multi-tasking is usually part of the routine, and multiple hats are worn in schools and in classrooms, for example, as teacher, advisor, mentor, administrator, lesson planner, classroom manager, support worker to name a few. Teaching is both a rewarding as well as an extremely challenging profession. Teachers' roles have increasingly become complex, requiring them to work with a diverse student population, an over-crowded curriculum using limited resources, dealing with parents and community, and still be expected to provide quality learning opportunities for students. In the absence of ongoing training, mentoring and other support mechanisms, high workload levels combined with stressful conditions in classrooms are known to result in emotional exhaustion, burn-out, ultimately leading to teacher attrition from the profession.

Psychological well-being consists of positive relationships with others, personal mastery, autonomy, a feeling of purpose and meaning in life, and personal growth and development. Psychological well-being is attained by achieving a state of balance affected by both challenging and rewarding life events.

Domains of Psychological Well-being

Self-acceptance

Which refers to the degree positive attitudes you have about yourself, your past behaviours and the choices that you have made. Someone with high self-acceptance is pleased with who they are and accepting of multiple aspects of themselves, both good and bad. In contrast, individuals with low self-acceptance are often self-critical, confused about their identity, and wish they were different in many respects.

Establishment of quality ties to others

An individual with positive relationships feels connected, respected, and well-loved. They can share aspects of themselves, experience intimacy, and usually feel secure in their relations. In contrast, individuals with poor relationships often feel unappreciated, disrespected, unloved, disconnected, hostile, rejected, or misunderstood. They tend to feel insecure and sometimes alone or distant from others.

Sense of autonomy

It refers individuals with high levels of autonomy are independent, self-reliant, can think for themselves, do not have a strong need to conform, and don't worry too much about what others think about them. In contrast, individuals low in autonomy feel dependent on others, are constantly worried about the opinions of others, are always looking to others for guidance, and feel strong pressures to conform to others' desires.

Mastery over the environment

Which is the degree to which you feel competent to meet the demands of your situation. Individuals high in environmental mastery feel they have the resources and capacities to cope, adjust and adapt to problems, and are not overwhelmed by stress. Those with a low level of environmental mastery may feel powerless to change aspects of their environment with which they are unsatisfied, feel they lack the resources to cope, and are frequently stressed or overwhelmed.

Personal growth

It refers individuals with high levels of personal growth see themselves as changing in a positive direction, moving toward their potential, becoming more mature, increasing their self-knowledge, and learning new skills. Individuals low in personal growth feel no sense of change or development, often feel bored and uninterested in life, and lack a sense of improvement over time.

Sense of purpose in life

It refers individual with a high sense of purpose sees their life has having meaning, they work to make a difference in the world, and often feel connected to ideas or social movements larger than themselves. Such individuals have a sense that they know what their life is about. Individuals low in this quality often question if there is a larger purpose, do not feel their life makes sense, and attribute no higher meaning or value to life other than the fulfilment of a series of tasks.

Importance of teacher well-being and management of stress

Even though teachers are used to new and uncertain situations, the pandemic has thrown a whole set of complex and unexpected challenges. Actions, based on medical advice, are needed to be swiftly understood and interpreted, appropriately implemented, and suitably communicated to students and their families. Learning methods and tools need modification, while adapting to students' individual needs and circumstances as best as possible. In the face of uncertainty around the pandemic, flexibility and the ability to shift between learning modes, with provision of appropriate support to students is key, but this is by no means an easy task. Remote working has substantially increased teachers' workload, with a recent study indicating that some teachers were working an extra 20 hours per week. Those who teach in low socio-economic or disadvantaged schools face additional barriers, having to perform their roles with less support and less resources, consequently compounding the existing challenges and inequities facing these school systems. Reduced opportunities for teachers to collaborate and work with colleagues is shown to impact their performance and commitment to the profession. The health and safety of teachers and their families is also a priority as they try and balance the different demands at work and home. Teachers are supporting their students, while also managing their own physical health, stress, anxiety, and supporting their family's needs. In addition to this, because women disproportionately represent the teaching profession, they are worse off during the pandemic due to the nature of their work as described above as well as having to be the primary career of their families, including caring for their children's health and educational needs. Being a woman and being a teacher during the pandemic has been a double whammy. Teachers' mental health and well-being can truly be tested, with far reaching implications both for themselves and for those under their care.

Teachers' mental health can no longer be ignored, and we need to do much better to prioritize the wellness and management of stress of teachers.

Strategies to consider

1. Encourage school colleagues and senior executive to collaboratively develop and design a teacher well-being plan including stress-management techniques.
2. Generate support from senior executive and leadership staff to recognise and acknowledge challenges and ongoing hurdles.

3. Apply adaptability and adjustment skills to current and future scenarios that maybe unfolding as a result of the pandemic.
4. Where available, enlisting the support of school psychologists and counsellors who have complementary and specialist skills, to communicate their feelings.
5. Recognize and accept uncertainty and what is achievable within the current situation.
6. Being part of or establishing supportive network of colleagues and friends within local community. Online teacher support groups can be useful to help gain a shared understanding of the causes of stress and suggestions to overcome them.
7. Wider community appreciation and valuing of teachers' professional roles to student contribution.

Healthy ways to cope with stress

- **Know** what to do if you are sick **and are concerned about COVID-19**. Contact a health professional before you start any self-treatment for COVID-19.
- **Know where and how to get treatment** and other support services and resources, including counselling or therapy.
- **Take care of your emotional health.** Taking care of your emotional health will help you think clearly and react to the urgent needs to protect yourself and your family.
- **Take breaks from watching, reading, or listening to news stories**, including those on social media. Hearing about the pandemic repeatedly can be upsetting.
- **Take care of your body**.
  - Take deep breaths, stretch.
  - Try to eat healthy, well-balanced meals.
  - Exercise regularly.
  - Get plenty of sleep.
  - Avoid excessive alcohol and drug use.

- **Make time to unwind**. Try to do some other activities you enjoy.
- **Connect with others**. Talk with people you trust about your concerns and how you are feeling.
- **Connect with your community- or faith-based organizations**. While social distancing measures are in place, consider connecting online, through social media, or by phone or mail.

Conclusion

Teachers make up a crucial component of the social fabric of our society. Our concern for schools and students during COVID-19 should also extend to teachers and their families. Failure to recognise and provide suitable support might leave some teachers vulnerable and unable to cope with their professional and personal demands, severely impacting their mental and physical health. Some might even be forced to re-consider leaving teaching, resulting in not just a huge loss to the profession and to students they teach, but will add to the current economic burden facing our society. So, there is a very important need of being psychological well and managing stress of the teacher.

References

https://www.cdc.gov/coronavirus/2019-ncov/daily-life-coping/managing-stress-anxiety.html

https://www.weareteachers.com/mental-health-during-covid/

https://smho-smso.ca/covid-19/educators/

https://www.csi.edu.au/media/uploads/csi_fact_sheet_teacherwellbeing.pdf

9
Impact of Lockdown on Mental Health of Pregnant Women: During COVID-19 Pandemic in the Barak Valley

Dipsikha Das

Introduction

People are now greatly cognizant about their heath in now-a-days especially during in this corona period. Different updates make people more wakeful regarding health and this is also followed in case of pregnant women also. They are now much more alert about their pregnancy than the earlier period. So, some kind of mental health diseases are faced by this section of women. Pregnancy period creates many experiences in women's life. During this period, they need extra care from their family members as well as from the society. But due to COVID-19, they are advised to maintain safe social distancing from the members of the society as well as from their relatives. From a survey it is observed that around 10 per cent of pregnant women suffer from mental disorder globally, mostly depression and it is even higher (16%) in developing nations (Zeng et al., 2020). So, pregnant women are not only at risk for medical related issues but also at risk for psychological problems mainly due to social distancing. During this critical period, they are not getting the support of their loved ones. Social distancing and other restrictions prevented them to attach with their relatives as well as neighbourhood. They need mental support in this time. Moreover, many pregnant women are unwilling to visit their doctors due to the fear of infection in the hospital. Thus, there are so many reasons of mental health problems among the pregnant women which are observed in our study.

The term 'Lockdown' had changed the whole situation. Pregnant women felt insecure about the life of their babies. They could not have faith upon the health service providers as well as their family members. Their main concern was only to protect their babies. So, these women took extra pressure on themselves and outcome of this was creation of other kinds of health disorders in their bodies. In pre-pandemic period, about 15 per cent of pregnant women are facing mental health issues, but now it has increased to 41 per cent (Health Report of India, 2020). They are now thinking about the financial crisis and other related issues of it. These things add extra burden upon them and their family and it affects the pregnant women both directly as well indirectly. Pregnant women are finding extremely difficult to seek care and treatment from health centers and providers when complete lockdown had forced throughout the country. So, in the study it is tried to find out the impact of complete lockdown upon the mental health of pregnant women in Barak Valley area of Assam and it is observed that they are challenging with different types of mental health problems.

Review of Literature

There are some works on the mental health of pregnant women aspect during COVID pandemic. Some of the literatures are reviewed in the following:

Ceulemans et al. (2021) aimed to assess the mental health status of pregnant and breastfeeding women during the pandemic, and to explore potential associations between depressive symptoms, anxiety, and stress and women's socio demographic, health, and reproductive characteristics. The multinational study reveals that high levels of depressive symptoms and generalized anxiety among pregnant and breastfeeding women during the COVID-19 outbreak. The study findings underline the importance of monitoring peri-natal mental health during pandemics and other societal crises to safeguard maternal and infant mental health.

Wang et al. (2021) has explained the impact of COVID-19 over the globe. Pregnant women are at risk of infection. The study examined the frequency of washing hands with soap and wearing face mask when going out, prevalence of depression and anxiety, and identified their associated factors among pregnant women during the early phase of COVID-19 outbreak in China.

Objectives of the Study

The study is based on the following objectives:

- To find out the impact of lockdown in COVID-19 pandemic upon the mental health of pregnant women.
- To find out the types of mental health problems as well as preventive measures which they have taken to overcome it.

Hypotheses

On the basis of the above mentioned objectives, the following hypotheses can be framed:

- Complete lockdown in COVID-19 has increased the mental health problems among the pregnant women.
- Pregnant women are facing different types of mental health problems and they have followed some preventive measures.

Methodology

The study is based on both primary data and secondary data. Basically, secondary data are collected from health department website, internet, Indian newspaper, News Bulletin of TV, different health journals, National Family Health Survey, District health Reports etc. Actually, a pilot survey has conducted to study the impact of lockdown in COVID-19 pandemic upon the mental health of pregnant women of three districts of Barak Valley, Assam. No specific statistical tools and techniques are used for the study. 150 pregnant women from urban area of three districts such as Cachar, Karimganj, and Hailakandi (50 from each district respectively) of Barak Valley are selected randomly. Some data are collected from door to door survey and some are from the entry point of the different health centres. By using simple percentage method the study has analyzed. Collected data are not categorized in specific age group or any religion or their pregnancy time period. The pregnant women are from different age group and also from different religion.

Results and Discussion

Lockdown and Its Impact on Mental Health of Pregnant Women

COVID-19 Pandemic brings an unforgettable experience for pregnant women. Both Central and State Governments are taking different measures to control this pandemic and announcement of complete Lockdown is one of them. Women face different types of health problems especially during pregnancy. It makes physical discomfort, weight gain, tiredness, fear of pain, depression, anxiety etc. But corona virus and its effect build extra nervousness among the pregnant women of the study area. Though the study is based on urban area and they are getting better health facilities, still mental problems remain same among all pregnant women. They are very much tensed by seeing the situation and also the news report in media. They understand that the situation is not favourable for all and their safety is under question mark. According to a report, "A woman in the eighth month of pregnancy died in an ambulance after running eight hospitals either referred her to another facility as she showed symptoms of COVID-19, or cited lack of beds." It shows the pathetic condition of our country. Another report flash the fact that when a woman has taken for delivery in the nearest health center she died on the delivery table due to depression. The doctor said that her blood pressure fluctuates frequently in delivery time. Her family also admits the fact that she has been suffering from depression in last few days due to COVID-19 pandemic. This incidence happened during lockdown period. There are so many examples which enlighten the negative impact of corona virus upon the pregnant women all-over India. The present study also supports the facts and more or less same situation is followed in the three districts of Barak Valley.

The current study tries to show the impact of lockdown in COVID-19 pandemic on the mental illness among pregnant women of Barak Valley. The result reflects that pregnant women are robustly affected due to corona virus. They are facing several types of mental illness due to lockdown and uncertain atmosphere. Table 9.1 shows the different types of mental illness among pregnant women and also suffering rate in Cachar, Karimganj and Hailakandi districts of Barak Valley due to Corona Virus pandemic.

Table 9.1: Mental Illness due to Lockdown in COVID-19 (in %)

Name of Districts	Depression (in %)	Anxiety (in %)	Bipolar Disorder (in %)	Stress (in %)	Fear about delivery (in %)	Insomnia (in %)	Distress (in %)
Cachar	85	70	48	95	76	85	90
Karimganj	82	63	45	98	85	88	88
Hailakandi	87	72	50	95	90	80	95

Source: Primary Survey, 2020.

From Table 9.1, it is observed that Stress is the most common mental disease among pregnant women in Cachar, Karimganj and Hailakandi districts. It is 95 per cent in Cachar, 98 per cent in Karimganj and again 95 per cent in Hailakandi district. The data also reflects that the pregnant women of almost all the districts of Barak Valley are severely challenged with different mental health issues.

It has been observed that the uncertainty surrounding COVID-19 has led to higher levels of depression among the pregnant women. They feel fear of infection for themselves, as well as their infants. The secondary data shows that 85-90 per cent women are suffering from this problem and the present study also supports the statistics of health department. From primary survey, it is found that isolation and social distancing are the most vital reasons for heavy depression among pregnant women.

During lockdown pregnant women thought that whether the situation will be like earlier or what will happen in future. This creates anxiety among them and it is a common problem during pregnancy period. The pandemic situation of locality directly and indirectly affects women. The pandemic does not make them stable. The report of Indian newspapers reveal that 60-67 per cent women are suffering from this problem. The primary survey also supports the statistics. 70 per cent pregnant women from Cachar, 63 per cent from Karimganj, and 72 per cent from Hailakandi districts are facing the anxiety problem during the lockdown period.

Bipolar disorder is a mental problem which pregnant women cannot identify. They are not much aware of this disease. This is a kind of problem where sometimes women feel higher energy in works and sometimes low. In India, 40-45 per cent pregnant women are facing this problem. Actually, they do not know why this happen. But during the pandemic, the rate has slightly increased and it become 50 per cent. By putting different types of questions, this problem was identified among the surveyed women. In Cachar 48 per cent, in Karimganj it is 45 per cent and 50 per cent pregnant women in Hailakandi district are facing this problem.

A pregnant woman during pregnancy period thought many negative things regarding their delivery and corona virus has increased their fear of delivery in double. This is an automatic incidence and nobody can deny it. The survey report says that women from Hailakandi (90%) district are most in number in comparison to Karimganj (85%) and Cachar (76%) districts.

Insomnia is another common problem among pregnant women. But due to COVID, sleeplessness and restlessness problems become more among the pregnant women and this is supported by the primary survey also. Table 9.1 shows that pregnant women from all the three districts of Barak Valley are facing this problem mostly due to uncertain situation (85%, 88%, and 80% from Cachar, Karimganj and Hailakandi districts respectively).

Women during pregnancy period feel sudden pain, anguish, sorrow etc., this is nothing but a kind of mental illness and it is called distress. Women are also suffering from this problem in the studied area. The report suggests that 90 per cent women from Cachar, 88 per cent from Karimganj and 95 per cent from Hailakandi districts are suffering from this problem (Table 9.1).

It can be, thus, said that women from all the districts are suffering from mental health problems severely during this Corona period and both the family members as well as the health service providers are helpless to reduce these mental health disorders. The finding supports the fact that complete lockdown has increased mental health problems among the pregnant women compared to the earlier situation (supported by secondary data). So it can be said that COVID-19 badly affects the pregnant women.

Preventive Measures

The doctors of the studied area suggested some preventive measures for the pregnant lady. There are some other forms of preventives they have taken to overcome mental illness in the lockdown period. Table 9.2 shows some of the preventive measures which they have taken to remove the mental health problem.

Table 9.2: Preventive Measures to Reduce Mental Illness (in %)

Name of Districts	Different Preventive Measures (In %)					
	Valid Information (In %)	Online Counselling (In %)	Proper sleeping time (In %)	Exercise (In %)	Keep touch with relatives (In %)	Reading books (In %)
Cachar	28	27	40	20	45	15
Karimganj	24	20	35	15	40	7
Hailakandi	18	13	33	8	32	2

Source: Primary Survey, 2020.

Table 9.2 states that pregnant women of studied area are not getting current updates regarding the COVID-19 situation. 20-30 per cent pregnant women of all-over India are aware of the fact that COVID-19 is nothing but a disease and it is curable. The report reveals that 70 per cent pregnant women are not aware of COVID-19. The study also supports the fact. Only 28 per cent women from Cachar district are aware of the fact that corona is nothing but a disease and it is curable with proper information. Awareness problem is mostly found in Hailakandi district (18%). The health service providers also try to give proper information and reduce mental illness. So, it is the most important measure by which mental problem can be reduced in some extent.

Online counselling is another vital preventive measure to solve mental health problem in our country. But very minimum percentage of pregnant women of studied area has taken online counselling from the health service providers. The rate is again very poor in Hailakandi district (13%) compared to other districts of Barak Valley (27% in Cachar & 20% in Karimganj respectively). If they have taken proper counselling on time most of them will get relaxation in this pandemic situation.

Various news reports reveal that sleeping has also reduced their depression. The primary survey supports the mentioned fact and 40 per cent, 35 per cent and 33 per cent (Cachar, Karimganj & Hailakandi respectively) pregnant women of three districts of Barak Valley agree on the fact that proper sleeping time helps them to be relaxed during lockdown period. They shared that this is the only time when no such uncertainty comes in their mind. So both doctors and other sources suggest taking sleep on time especially in this time.

Other preventive measures such as exercise, keeping touch with friends and relatives, and reading books are also very helpful to solve the problem of mental illness among the pregnant women. The study reveals that 30-40 per cent pregnant women are doing exercise in the three districts of Barak Valley to reduce their stress problem. It is a good thing for their health. When they maintain relation with their friends and relatives via phone, it also reduces their stress and it is also supported by the study (Table 9.2).

Thus, it can be said that through these preventive measures mental health problem can be solved in the studied area and some of them are following these measures also.

Suggestions

Throughout the study, it is observed that pregnant women are suffering from different types of mental illness in Barak Valley. So to improve the mental health status in this pandemic situation, some suggestive measures are mentioned below:

- Meditation and regular exercise is needed.
- Family support is also important.
- Regular counselling is must.
- Supply valid information regarding COVID-19.
- Nutritious food is also very necessary because proper diet also reduces mental health problems.
- Keeping in touch with relatives.

Conclusion

The problem of mental health of women is multidimensional and complex in India and this COVID-19 pandemic brings it in light. The Government of India had announced an immediate and total lockdown on 24 March, 2020, which was extended to 31 May, 2020. This has badly impacted the economic condition of the people. Though government has tried to do their best in this situation, but somehow it does not work and our economy is now in a very crucial condition. The study shows that lockdown in COVID-19 increases mental health problems among pregnant women and so some of the preventive measures are used to confiscate mental health problems.

It is necessary that health service providers should give attention to pregnant women to reduce possible symptoms of depression. Detecting and treating of depression in the beginning could prevent detrimental long term effects on maternal and infant health.

References

Zeng Liang-Nan, Chen Li-Gang, Chang Mei-Yang, Zeng Li-Ping (2020). Mental Health Care for Pregnant Women in the COVID-19 Outbreak in Urgently Needed. Women Birth, 4th May 2020, Elsevier Public Health Emergency Collection, www.ncbi.nlm.nih.gov.

Ceulemans M., Foulon V., Ngo E. (2021). "Mental health status of pregnant and breastfeeding women during the COVID-19 pandemic—A multinational cross-sectional study." Retrieved from: https://doi.org/10.1111/aogs.14092.

Wang Q., K.H. Mo. P., Song B. (2021). "Mental health and preventive behaviour of pregnant women in China during the early phase of the COVID-19 period." *Infectious Diseases of Poverty*, 37 (2021). Retrieved from: https://idpjournal.biomedcentral.com.

Report of News Channels of India.

Report of Newspaper of India.

Report of Health Department of India.

News report from Barak Valley.

SECTION-III

COVID-19 AND ITS IMPACT ON MARGINALISED GROUPS

10
Working Women's Life during COVID-19 Lockdown in Guwahati City: A Study from Gender Perspective

Priyanka Gogoi and *Mercy Hazarika*

Introduction

Corona virus is a newly identified infectious disease caused by a novel coronavirus reported first in Wuhan Municipal Health Commission, China (WHO, 2020). The COVID-19 virus has spread globally and was declared as pandemic by the World Health Organisation (WHO) on 11th March, 2020. Subsequently, it spread to other parts of China and then globally. The first COVID-19 case in India was identified in Kerala on 30th January, 2020 and within two months the number of positive cases started growing because of international travellers and tourists (Belfin et al., 2020). As a result, a national lockdown was declared on 24th March, 2020 for 21 days which was extended later to stop further spread. In Assam, the first case got detected on the 31st of March, 2020 amidst the national lockdown in Silchar Medical College and since then the number is rising although the rate is considerably under control now.

The pandemic has affected the world in all spheres and on all grounds, be it the global economy, the society, health, environment, politics or education. It has become one of the biggest threats to the human race post the 2nd World War. People were confined to their homes and had to adapt to working from home. Many had to compromise with their salary whereas some had to compromise with their jobs. Work from home was announced as an alternative to carry on the necessary work. Work from home is still a very new concept considering Assam being a 'not so' tech savvy State on an average count.

As said earlier, the motive behind announcing lockdown was to stop the spread of community transmission and minimizing the number of COVID-19 positive cases. Every individual faced a lot of hurdles during lockdown. However, some people have seen the worst as they lost their source of income, especially informal workers. On the other hand, if we look at the life of a man and a woman then the report published by the United Nations (UN) shows that women become more vulnerable as some women are being forced to lockdown at home with their abusers. At the same time, the service to domestic violence support survivors is being inaccessible or disrupted because of COVID-19 pandemic (UN, 2020). Along with the UN report, a recent study also found that there are rising reported cases of domestic violence as couples and families are bound to stay together because of the lockdown which again has put women at a greater risk (Taub, 2020). The National Commision for Women (NCW) stated that in 2020, complaints related to domestic violence, cyber crime, harassment, rape, dowry-related complaints, police apathy against women, as well as trafficking and prostitution of women made up more than 90 per cent of total complaints received by the NCW. It is also found that the ability to keep stable employment is affected for years after the experience of domestic violence, likely as the result of health ramifications stemming from the abuse, leaving victims financially vulnerable and with limited resources (Crowne et al., 2011).

Along with this, there are ample studies on gender inequalities in household chores and work family conflict (Noonan, 2001) (Cerrato & Cifre, 2018). Studies find that individuals may affect or experience conflict between work and home role due to limited time, over workload both in the workplace and home that may lead to high levels of stress. To understand the work-home conflict it is essential to understand how gender plays a significant role in an individual's life (Wood and Eagly, 2010). Whether it is Indian society or Western society, one can observe gender based division of labour in every household. A study conducted to understand gender based division of labour found that most of the household chores are assumed to be a woman's responsibility. Household chores such as washing, ironing, shopping, cooking, or cleaning etc. are considered as women's responsibility. It clearly shows how much it is difficult to balance work-life for a woman. According to D. Babin Dhas (2000), "Work-life balance is about creating and maintaining supportive and healthy work environments, which will enable employees to have balance between work and personal responsibilities and thus strengthen employee loyalty and productivity" (p. 2). Several researchers have concluded that there is a profound interlocking relationship between work-life and private life (Johnson & Gardner, 1999; McFerran, 2011b; Murray & Powell, 2007; Swanberg & Macke, 2006; Swanberg & Logan, 2005; Tolman, 2011). But the question here is—whether a woman would be able to maintain work-life balance? Being a woman it is difficult to maintain work-life balance as working women are overburdened by household chores even in normal days. So, how do they manage work-life balance while working from home? What kind of challenges do they face during COVID-19 lockdown? This study was an attempt to get answers to these questions through a qualitative study.

Research Objectives

Objective of the research was to understand the working women's life during COVID-19 lockdown.

Research Questions

1. How did the working women maintain work-life balance during the pandemic?
2. How was the distribution of household work during COVID-19 lockdown?

Methodology

Qualitative research design was used to conduct the research. The study was conducted in Guwahati city of Assam. The area of the study was selected conveniently as the situation does not permit the researcher to travel to other places. Both primary and secondary data was used to conduct the study. Narrative approach was used to collect primary data for which an interview guide was used while books, journals and government and non-government websites were used to collect secondary data. The primary data has been conducted both face to face and telephonic interview.

Snowball and purposive sampling has been used to draw sampling. The researchers have used snowball sampling as it is difficult to access the working women personally due to movement restrictions set by the Government of India. The data has been collected during the first week of August, 2020. The sample size is 10. The inclusive criterion of sampling is working women in the formal sector.

Result and Findings

After finishing the data collection process, the interviews of the respondents were transcribed and then, it was analysed thematically. The result and findings of the study will be discussed here briefly.

Household work

Household work generally includes cleaning, washing, cooking and the entire management of the house. The society has a preconceived notion that all household chores are to be done by women alone which is not different in case of working women too. Women are not left with a choice to choose between one. In this regard, an assistant professor named M. Choudhary describes her situation by comparing it with a pendulum. When she was asked how she had spent her lockdown, she said, *"Swing like a pendulum between work and home"* (mother of a 3 year old child). It clearly shows how much it is difficult for a woman to manage work from home.

Talking about household responsibilities, it is difficult to generalise that every woman needs to take household responsibility. A woman working in an NGO, unmarried and 27 years old said,

> *"My mother does all the household work. I am glad that I do not need to take any household responsibility. She only managed groceries and all during the lockdown period. Therefore, I did not face any difficulties to do work from home. Yes, but sometimes my mother asked me to chop vegetables while attending online meetings... (laughing loud). That's it. I only do online payments such as TV recharge, mobile recharge, payment of electricity bill etc".*

Another respondent, who is a 32 year old unmarried woman and a HR manager in a reputed media house said,

> *"I just had the pressure of office work as I work for a media house and there is no time-table even if a said one was given. I am glad that I am unmarried and don't have to maintain the house. Else, the lockdown would have made me go crazy. I never felt the need for distribution as my mother was always doing her duty, she remarked with a smirk".*

The statements made above clearly indicate that unmarried women had less pressure of household work on them. The second statement made by the HR professional somewhere depicts that maintaining the house is thought to be the sole responsibility of the mother alone.

Overburden of work

Adaption of a new concept, i.e., work from home is left as one and only option to carry our work and life smoothly as well as to save the global economy. However, some of the respondents said that it was overburdened for them because they had to deal with both work and home simultaneously. Along with this, this study reveals that because of not maintaining a proper time-table creates a lot of hurdle in an individual's life.

> *"Initially, I was getting bored staying at home. But once the online classes have been started I am not getting time for me. Though the working hour is from 9AM to 5 PM but in actual we work more than that. One thing I have noticed is that there is no specific time for coming notification. Sometimes we get notifications or circular at 11.30 or 12 AM. There were incidents of attending meetings from 8 PM at night. Work from home is really difficult"* —K. Phukon, 29 years old

The above discussion reveals how it is difficult to maintain a work-life balance as the women are already overloaded by household chores. And when women adapt work from home concept to adjust with new normal, they face a lot of difficulties especially a married woman with a child. In this regard, a woman who have a girl child explained that,

> *"Yes, I worked from home. I managed because I had no choice! I scheduled my professional and personal time and duties. Indeed it was difficult and 100 times more hectic. It affected me physically."*

Work-life Balance

Maintaining work-life balance is requisite to minimise the work home conflict. The studies show that a woman faces lots of hurdles to manage the balance between work and home as women are assumed to be a caretaker of the whole family. In this society where people have a patriarchal mindset, it becomes more difficult for a woman to balance between work and home, especially when the whole world is adapting to working from home. As the women do not have any choice they have to manage it in some way. One of the respondents opined that,

> *"Yes, I am lucky enough to have my husband sharing the load willingly, the only difference being that when he works from home, he has the liberty to sit with the laptop for hours without disturbance or any other responsibilities. But, when I work from home, sitting for hours and working peacefully becomes a luxury. I have to multitask all the time."*

She uses the term 'multitasker' which means managing many tasks at the same times. Regarding managing many tasks at the same time, one respondent described it very nicely. She said,

> *"When I have online class, my daughter and son also have their online class. So, it is really difficult for me to manage. My son reads in class four so he needs me sometimes while attending online classes though my daughter could handle everything by her own as she is in HS first year. And I stay alone with my children as my husband stays in a different place because of work purpose. The part-time helper also could not come because of the lockdown".*

Health issue (Physical and mental)

Though it is good to hear about work from home as people do not need to go to the workplace physically but in reality it is not so easy and very convenient. It was already discussed how work from home became overburdened for women as they had to manage between work and home. At the same time, analysis of the respondents' response also indicates that overburdened work from home occurred because of not maintaining a gap between a private and professional space. Not only it creates work home conflict but also it affects the health of an individual physically as well as psychologically. One of the key factors of physical unwellness is sitting constantly in front of a screen to complete official works, attend meetings, or to take classes. Everything has to be done on an online platform that affects the health. In this context, one respondent who is 28 years old, professionally a teacher said,

> *"I even had health issues like back pain, headache due to long continuous hours of working on the laptop. The pressure was extremely different from normal working days and it strained my personal relationship to a good extent."*

The above statement clearly shows that the respondent was suffering from back pain and headache. In addition to this, some of the respondents said that they were also suffering from eye rashes because of looking at the laptop or mobile screen for a long period of time. Moreover, the statement of the respondent also reveals how much this pandemic was stressful. Here, the research would like to quote two statements of respondent which clearly depicts the stressful life that they were living.

> *"Yes, since 23rd March, online classes for students started and since then there is no looking back for us. Although timing for work was 10 a.m. to 4 p.m., there was no proper timetable. At times I felt overburdened with work and became frustrated and angry."* (B. Hazarika, 29 years old)

> *"Yes, working from home is way different than working from the office. We realised that working from home has no static time limit and hence it really affected me physically and mentally as there is no relaxation.* (T. Das, 34 years old)

So, from the analysis of the data, we have found that working women were facing lots of difficulties because of not having a proper working timetable, not having a private space to work, overloaded household responsibility. Moreover, continuous use of laptops leads to health issues such as back pain, headache, eye rashes and stress.

Discussion

After thematic analysis of the primary data, major findings of study will be discussed.

Gender based division of labour

In the introductory part itself, it was discussed how gender inequalities in distributing household chores prevails in our society (Noonan, 2001) (Cerrato & Cifre, 2018). Gender Division of Labour is the result of how each society distributes work among men and among women according to what is considered appropriate to each gender (March et al., 1999). This study also discussed the distribution of household chores on the basis of gender. Taking care of children is the prime responsibility of the woman though; husband and other family members extend their helping hands. Along with taking care of children, other household chores especially, cooking, washing and cleaning are mainly done by women. The study, however, shows that male members of the family also enter the kitchen and prepare delicious dishes and help the wife. But, one thing that we could not ignore is that the male members do the work according to their choice whereas women aren't left with any.

Whenever we discuss the definition of Empowerment by The World Bank, it defines empowerment as the "expansion of freedom of choice and action to shape one's life". But the findings and analysis depicts a contrary picture of the definition. One could raise the question on "whether an economically empowered woman is also socially empowered?" This study shows that an economically empowered woman may not be empowered socially. Though, now-a-days a few women have the freedom of deciding whether she will work or not, but at the same time, the same women may not get the freedom to decide whether she will do household chores or not. But, we can refer to a woman as completely empowered only when she is socially, economically and politically empowered. As they are not empowered as a whole therefore during lockdown, some women especially, married and women with children faced lots of difficulties to handle work from home as there is lack of private space to work without any disturbance.

Gender awareness Vs. gender sensitization

Gender awareness refers to the ability to view society from the perspective of gender roles and understand how it has affected women's needs in comparison to the needs of men (Paterna et al., 2010). On the other hand, gender sensitization means modification of behaviour by raising awareness to bring gender equality (Rajashree, 2016). Parents and teachers play significant roles in modification of behaviour and acquiring gender equality. One could raise questions on "people who are aware of gender inequalities and other gender issues, are they also gender sensitized?" "do they share household chores equally without distributing it based on gender?"

The earlier discussion of gender based division of labour indicates that gender inequality directly or indirectly prevails in all patriarchal societies. This study was conducted among the women who work in formal settings who are highly qualified and their partners too. Still, we can see gender inequality or gender based division of labour in case of most of the respondents. We should not forget that men are born and brought up in a patriarchal society. Therefore, though they are aware about the issues related to gender and gender inequality still, it takes time to be sensitized completely.

Double burdened

There are ample numbers of studies conducted on the double burden of women. The term "double burden" refers to characterizing the difficulties that a woman faces while balancing work and household responsibilities. Studies reveal that the level of burden of a woman keeps changing with the transition of age (Massey et al., 1995). An unmarried woman has less responsibility or household responsibility than a married woman. On the other hand, a married woman with a child has more burden on their shoulder as she needs to take care of the child. When children grow, this burden could lessen, however, transition to grandmother could increase the responsibility again. This study also comes with a similar finding. This present study clearly shows that a married woman with a child has more household responsibilities than an unmarried woman. Therefore, they face lots of difficulties to manage working from home, especially when children are young and they are also attending school from home. Taking care of children, doing all the household chores, helping them attend online class and examinations, and helping them to submit homework online along with her own job responsibility is beyond manageable. Still, the working women with children are doing as they do not have any other choices.

However, this study also shows that a working woman could lessen her burden by keeping a caretaker or helper. A respondent who has a full time caretaker did not face much difficulty as her household work was shared with the caretaker. But, it could not be possible during COVID-19 lockdown if someone wants to keep part-time housekeeper or caretaker. That is why we can say that working women with children face double burden of work during the lockdown period.

Recommendation and conclusion

The study reveals that gender inequality and gender based division of labour still prevails in the society for which a working woman becomes overburdened as she needs to handle all the household chores. And talking about work from home, it was more difficult for a working woman to manage the balance between home and work because of not having private space to work as they were occupied by other household chores. Married working women and women with children are more overburdened as they need to take more responsibility.

Considering the above issue, to reduce the workload of working women, the head or manager of the working place needs to manage an appropriate time schedule which should not exceed 9 hours as the standard time for employees is 8 hours. It will let a working woman give equal time to both home and work. Along with this, gender sensitization is required to reduce the burden of a working woman and it will also give a woman to enjoy her work fully without any stress and guilt.

The researchers would like to give recommendations on which further study can be carried out. Firstly, further study can be done using mixed methods research which will help the researcher in data triangulation. Secondly, one could carry out a study on domestic violence during lockdown which was not touched in this study because of the limited time period. Thirdly, one could carry a study on women's life working in the informal sector as this study could not cover the informal works because of restriction on movement.

References

Belfin, R.V. (2020, January 1). COVID-19 peak estimation and effect of nationwide lockdown in India. Retrieved August 17, 2020, from https://www.medrxiv.org/content/10.1101/2020.05.09.20095919v1

Cerrato, J., & Cifre, E. (2018b, August 3). Gender Inequality in Household Chores and Work-Family Conflict. Retrieved August 19, 2020, from https://www.frontiersin.org/articles/10.3389/fpsyg.2018.01330/full

Crowne, S.S., Juon, H.S., Ensminger, M., Burrell, L., McFarlane, E., & Duggan, A. (2010). "Concurrent and Long-Term Impact of Intimate Partner Violence on Employment Stability." *Journal of Interpersonal Violence, 26*(6), 1282-1304. https://doi.org/10.1177/0886260510368160

Johns Hopkins University. (2020). COVID-19 Map. Retrieved August 20, 2020, from https://coronavirus.jhu.edu/map.html

Johnson, P. R., & Gardner, S. (1999). "Domestic violence and the workplace: developing a company response." Journal of Management Development, 18(7), 590-597. https://doi.org/10.1108/02621719910284440

March, C., Smyth, I., & Mukhopadhyay, M. (1999). A Guide to Gender-Analysis Frameworks. Retrieved August 23, 2020, from https://oxfamilibrary.openrepository.com/handle/10546/115397

Massey, G., Hahn, K., & Sekulić, D. (1995). "Women , Men , and the 'Second Shift' in Socialist Yugoslavia." Gender & Society, 9(3), 359-379. https://doi.org/10.1177/089124395009003006

McFerran, L. (2011). "Why domestic violence is a workplace issue." *Parity, 24*(8), 36

Noonan, M.C. (2001). "The Impact of Domestic Work on Men's and Women's Wages." *Journal of Marriage and Family, 63*(4), 1134-1145.https://doi.org/10.1111/j.1741-3737.2001.01134.x

Martínez, C., Paterna, C., Roux, P., & Falomir, J.M. (2010). "Predicting gender awareness: the relevance of neo-sexism." Journal of Gender Studies, 19(1), 1-12. https://doi.org/10.1080/09589230903057142

Rajashree. (2016). "Gender Sensitization – Equality of Opportunity in Indian Context Education." *Indian Journal of Research, 5*(10). https://www.researchgate.net/publication/308899434%0AGender

Swanberg, J.E., & Macke, C. (2006). "Intimate Partner Violence and the Workplace." Affilia, 21(4), 391-406. https://doi.org/10.1177/0886109906292133

Swanberg, J.E., & Logan, T.K. (2005). "Domestic Violence and Employment: A Qualitative Study." Journal of Occupational Health Psychology, 10(1), 3-17. https://doi.org/10.1037/1076-8998.10.1.3

Tolman, R. (2011). "Impact of intimate partner violence on economic well-being." CFS Research Brief, 5, 1-5, https://centerforfinancialsecurity.files.wordpress.com/2015/04/tolman2011.pdf

United Nations Entity for Gender Equality and the Empowerment of Women (UN Women). (2020, April 9). Policy brief: The impact of COVID-19 on women. Retrieved August 1, 2020, from https://asiapacific.unwomen.org/en/digital-library/publications/2020/04/policy-brief-the-impact-of-covid-19-on-women

WHO. (2020). Coronavirus. Retrieved August 15, 2020, from World Health Organisation: https://www.who.int/health-topics/coronavirus#tab=tab_1

Wood, W., & Eagly, A.H. (2010). "Gender." In S.T. Fiske, D.T. Gilbert, & G. Lindzey (Eds.), *Handbook of Social Psychology* (pp. 629-667). John Wiley & Sons, Inc.. https://doi.org/10.1002/9780470561119.socpsy001017

11
Violence against Women in India with Special Reference to the State of Assam: The Shadow Pandemic

Karavi Barman

Introduction

The significance of the 'home' in a women's life and the paradox that surrounds it is aptly reflected in the words—

The "Home" is Ideologically understood as a place of safety and refuge.
Such an account cloaks violence against women.
The voices of battered women can disrupt
That dominant construction of the space of the home,
A construction typified by the work of Gaston Bachelard.
The space that Bachelard presupposes and theorizes as
Given is in fact being-produced, cleaned, and organized by people who themselves may not find in it any solace or respite (Price, 2020).

Domestic Violence is a health, legal, economic, educational, development and, above all, human rights issue. The World Conference on Human Rights held in Vienna, explicitly recognized a gender-specific rights violations including violence against women through the UN Declaration on the Elimination of Violence against Women through UN Declaration Convention known as the Vienna Declaration. In contemporary times, domestic violence against women is the most sensational and complex issue as it directly hints the sanctity of the Indian family system. Domestic Violence affects its victims in many ways. It has both short term and long term effects. Domestic Violence affects all aspects of women's lives—physical, psychological, economic and others.

COVID-19 pandemic has led to double the gender based cases in the country and the upward trend of violence against women is deeply disturbing the social equilibrium at large. The pandemic has put a drastic havoc to the mark in the society adversely affecting the many vulnerable sections of the society and the horrifying aspects of this lockdown which was started on March 23rd is the Domestic Violence of women, a shadow pandemic which has taken toll on most of the women as the facts and figures of the National Commission for Women reveal that there has been a sharp increase in cases thereby shifting the females to the position from where they rose up after years of struggle.

This chapter highlights how domestic violence by the husbands and their interpersonal complexity is addressed within the legal framework of the special beneficial legislation of protection of Women from Domestic Violence Act. The study further provides an in-depth analysis into the gap existing between the Act and its implementation in reality in India, especially in the state of Assam.

Operational Definitions of the Key Concepts

Human Rights:

Human Rights are the basic rights and freedoms that belong to every person in the world, from birth until death. These basic rights are based on shared values like dignity, fairness, equality, respect and independence.

Gender Based Violence:

Gender-based violence is a serious, life-threatening protection issue primarily affecting women and children. It is well documented that GBV is a widespread international public health and human rights issue, and adequate, appropriate, and comprehensive prevention and response are inadequate in most countries.

Domestic Violence:

Domestic violence is a pattern of coercive, controlling behaviour that is a pervasive life-threatening crime affecting people in all our communities specially the womenfolk.

Objectives of the study

The study is aimed to achieve the following objectives—

(i) to analyze the perspectives of women and the perpetrators of domestic violence especially in view of the pandemic scenario.

(ii) to illustrate the standpoint of the stakeholders thereby making an attempt to develop a holistic approach.

(iii) to educate the masses regarding the provisions under which they could take shield.

(iv) to suggest policy measures with a note to end this gender based violence in the state.

(v) to bring about an awareness in the society thereby bring about end to this gruesome evil.

Problem Statement

About sixty nine cases were reported in India from 24th March to 4th April and this is quite an increase in the number than the normal period. The chapter is a humble attempt to highlight the very fact that women in rural as well as in urban scenario are silent sufferers as they are ignorant of the rights provided to them under the Domestic Violence Act, 2005, a beneficial legislation to safeguard them from the atrocities of the patriarchal stereo-typical cultural phenomena. The crux is to bring into forefront the vital issues that despite the provisions in the Act, there are many pitfalls when it comes to the part of implementation.

Methodology

The study is based on both primary and secondary data. Primary data were collected from the survivors of domestic violence who registered their cases under Section 498-A IPC or PWDVA, 2005 and from the judicial officers and protection officers in Assam. Interview method was used to get the information about the registered cases and the opinions of the protection officers in this respect. Pseudo-names have been used to protect the identity of the victims. In addition interview was conducted with some stakeholders to get an insight and explore the area extensively.

The secondary data were collected from the books and journals including the newspaper clipping that have depicted a shabby picture of the women not only in the rural areas but also in the urban areas of Assam. Both qualitative and quantitative methods were employed in probing the vital issue.

Review of literature

In a report entitled 'Domestic Violence in India—a summary report of Three Studies', written in September 1999, Leela Visaria dealt extensively with the studies of violence against women in India—Evidence from Rural Gujarat where she described the various instances pertaining the incidents of woman in rural Gujarat. This research programme in India is part of the larger global grants programme called promoting women in development being implemented by ICRW in partnership with CEDPA and funded by USAID.

Nishi Mitra in "Best Practices among Responses to Domestic Violence in Maharastra and Madhya Pradesh", narrated various incidents from records of villages. The data instruments from the large study investigated the relationship between women's education and autonomy, their health seeking behaviour and management of illness suffered by their children and their treatment seeking behaviour regarding their own gynecological problems. She went further in suggesting suitable measures for betterment of the womenfolk.

In the same report, Veena Poonanacha and Divya Pandey, in 'Responses to Domestic Violence in Karnataka and Gujarat' dealt with the evidences of the women suffering with no ready solution in the states of Karnataka and Gujarat. She has particularly stressed on the family counselling cells in some interior places. She further stressed on the opening of shelter homes and short stay homes. In addition, support groups could be of help thereby assisting the women in breaking the shackles and free them from violence against them.

Shreya Bhandari and Jennifer C. Hughes in the article 'Lived Experiences of Women Facing Domestic Violence in India', described about the lived experiences of domestic violence victims among a convenience sample of 21 low income Indian women. This article illustrates the various crimes against women suffering from domestic violence in the state.

Sharon Prescila, in the article entitled 'Domestic Violence in India: A Family Menace' discussed at length about the different effects of violence on the victims and family and further stressed on the various recommendations for curbing the menace.

International Perspectives

The worrying phenomena is not only in India but also world-wide. This is just one side of the picture and the other side is something out of imagination as the rural women are the worst sufferers not even knowing about many operation mechanisms.

In United States there has been a significant increase in the number of cases to 20 per cent. In Turkey, there has been 38.2 per cent increase in the cases where the women are not only tortured but murdered. Ninety thousand gender based cases have been reported in South Africa. The National Domestic Abuse helpline in United Kingdom has witnessed 25 per cent increase. The Australian Government has reported 75 per cent increase in online searches for support in Domestic Violence.

UK, however had started its campaign against the domestic violence by providing boot shops. They have allocated small areas which are put up as counselling centres and if anyone goes to buy something they can go to that corner and narrate the woes as somebody will instantly be present their to provide assistance and can get the complain registered and go back home safe.

In France, there has been a rise in the number of cases to 32 per cent in the first week of the nationwide lockdown itself. Antonio Guterres, UN Secretary General appealed that the matter should be treated urgently as the local support groups are paralysed in the countries due to shortage of funds. He urged that all the governments should take up redressal mechanisms.

In France, there were hotels opened for the survivors along with the pop up of twenty counselling centres in shops like grocery shops, pharmacies and so forth. The women can get help while successfully rescue herself in the name of moving out to purchase groceries as those shops are instructed to help the victims. In Spain, the pharmacies were instructed to help any lady seeking help in distress and if at all she turned up with her abuser a code word 'mask 19' was to be asked and everything could be understood by the chemist and he would immediately connect to the authorities.

In San Francisco, there was sixty per cent increase in the cases of domestic violence. A number of causes during this time has remained constant and becomes more complicated. Initiatives were taken by the city to make alternate means for safety planning of the domestic violence survivors to stay for ninety days with no cost. Twenty furnished apartments were secured for the survivors. The temporary arrangements are located in the several secured buildings throughout the city and toll free number '911' is available to the victims for call for help. This is an incredible toll as it is quite known that if anyone is attacked or physically abused it is definitely difficult to reach out for help.

In Italy, in grocery shops, the counselling centres are established to provide relief to the victims of domestic violence.

Indian Scenario

The woes of Indian couples are no less with stay at home orders where the Domestic violence cases have soared up and living abusive partners is becoming a nightmare for them. The state governments are not taking initiatives especially in the time of pandemic as it is not within the ambit of essential services. The police are advising the victims to bear with these in silence as they are overburdened with their daily task. To get relief the first thing is to step out of the house but in India there are no safety locations provided for the survivors. What is witnessed is that there are no safety homes provided at this hour for them. No advertisements are done about this situation in our country.

The people in India have learnt to be tolerant and are not fighting against the system. The government at this hour is trying to fight the pandemic based on speculations and hence it is the stakeholders who need to walk the last mile and combat the grave gender based violence.

Highlights on the Domestic Violence Act, 2005

What is Domestic Violence?

For the purpose of the Act, Section 3 provides that, any act, omission or commission or conduct of the respondent shall constitute domestic violence in case it—

(a) harms or injures or endangers the health, safety, limb or well-being, whether mental or physical, of the aggrieved person or tends to do and includes causing physical abuse, sexual abuse, verbal and emotional abuse and economic abuse; or

(b) harasses, harms, injures or endangers the aggrieved person with a view to coerce her any other person related to her to meet any unlawful demand for any dowry or other property or valuable security; or

(c) has effect of threatening the aggrieved person or any other person related to her by any conduct; or

(d) otherwise injuries or causes harm, whether physical or mental, to the aggrieved person.

Who is entitled to the protection under the DV Act, 2005?

The Act seeks to cover those women who are or have been in a relationship with the abuser where both parties have lived together in a shared household and are related by consanguinity, marriage or a relationship in the nature of marriage, or adoption; in addition relationship with family members living together as a joint family are also included. Even those women who are sisters, widows, mothers, single mother, or living with them are entitled to get protection under the Act.

Aim of the Act

The aim of the Act is to protect the women from any form of Domestic violence. It covers all forms of mental and physical torture endured by the women along with verbal threats made to them.

For the purpose of the Act certain authorities are set up

Protection Officers and Shelter Homes find direct mention in the Act.

Striking features of the Act

- Four types of abuse included— emotional, mental, physical and verbal.

- Even taunting and humiliation or passing caustic comments are included within the ambit.
- Women's right to secure housing.
- Power of the court to pass protection orders preventing the abuser from indulging in unwarranted acts.
- Appointment of Protection officers.
- Shelter Homes for protection of the victims.
- Protection in regard to medical expenses, legal aid and safe shelter.

Analysis of two cases: Evidence from Nagoan and Morigaon districts of Assam

Case Study I

A lady named Radha, in the Nagoan District of Assam was strangulated by her in-laws within just one year of her marriage. She was an educated lady and the main problem was the inferiority complex of the in-laws. She used to work as a school teacher there but her in-laws used to torture her on trivial issues like – food not cooked properly, stained on the clothes remained and so forth. She made repeated complaints to her parents but they wanted her to stay and adjust in the family and also used to console her stating that the day is not to far when things would fall in the place. But, things worsened to such a state that one day they killed her.

Arpana Kindo, a labour Inspector in the Kaliabor District observed that – Domestic Violence can be controlled and stopped by the victim herself if she raises her voice of protest against this evil. Moreover, she said that educated women should utilize their empowerment as a tool to rescue even other victims and act as support system to the illiterate class. Domestic violence could also be curbed by bringing changes at home and the patriarchal attitude should be changed first. Moreover, she stated that it is a sheer necessity to change the negative mindset of the society. She also said that in most cases, the abuser thinks that it is his right to beat or slap his wife and the lady thinks that she is destined to it.

The researcher happened to collect some data from the **protection Officer of that District, Dinesh Das**. He expressed his concern over the fact that they were heavily burdened with responsibilities and so could not take up much of the cases of Domestic Violence which multiplied in times of the pandemic. He said that due to the non-functioning of the courts except on some urgent matters, the victims turned out to be the worst sufferers. He said that despite being the protection officer, he was also acting in the capacity of District Programme Officer and District Social Welfare Officer and hence he was overburdened. He opined that there should be appointment of officers only for the rescue of the victims of domestic violence but the problem as a whole was given a blind folded approach.

Case Study II

A lady, named Savita was thrown out of her matrimonial home by her in-laws in the Morigaon District of Assam as her husband left her and went to work in Kerala but he stopped sending money and when court passed order against him, he never turned up and even his whereabouts were known to none. Her friend stated that even if the magistrate passed order in her favour but it was an ex-parte order which remain unexecuted.

It was observed by the researcher that in most of the cases ex-parte orders were given which were confined to papers only.

Sushmita Goswami, Bureau Chief, United News of India, Guwahati observed—The COVID-19 pandemic and consequent lockdown has led to shrinkage of income and even loss of livelihood altogether. Also, it has led to confinement within home for a long period without any time to mentally condition oneself for such an extended indoor stay, with abrupt halt of all normal activities. Such factors lead to mental anxiety and even mental problems, with the children, aged and women becoming vulnerable to abuse at the hands of the male members, whose life have been more hit by the lockdown. With no means to seek succor and ignorant mostly of their own mental state, the male members tend to lash out at their wives, sisters, daughters and even mothers. Lack of contribution to the family in monetary terms by the female members become a source of taunt for them and gets to the stage of physical abuse at times. The uncertainty created by the pandemic has also thrown the people off gear, and this could manifest in increased abuse of female members with the male members resorting to it as a means of unwinding their own anxieties.

Rekha Sharma, National Commission for Women stated in a webinar that she has been receiving many complaints in their website including personal mails. She viewed that the complaints belonged to different genre because of the lockdown and the women are not being able to reach the police due to the fearsome scenario existing in their mindset that if at all the husband happens to know about the complain, the picture might turn even more devastating.

Rajinder Pal Kaur, President of Sitapur in Uttar Pradesh shared her personal experience with the researcher via telephonic conversation. She stated that condition in U.P. was also terrible when it comes to the gender sensitive issues and she herself had suffered a nightmare as her own daughter, an highly qualified, and a recipient of governor's award was killed by her in-laws over trivial issues and one of the issue was that she wanted to work and establish her identity. However, she left her job but in vain as the torture multiplied. Mrs Kaur herself suffered a lot as she had to move from pillar to post seeking for justice.

Findings of the Study

- **Social Stigma and Superstitions are the root causes of the non-utilization of the Domestic Violence Act by the Survivors.** From the narratives of the victim, it was observed that even if they were aware of the legal provisions of the DVA, 2005, they did not take the risk of complaining on account of fear of being stigmatized from the kith and kin. And when it comes to educated women, they were more concerned in protecting their reputation in their workplaces. Moreover, in rural areas some even believed that they were destined to such exploitation from their spouses.
- **Protection Officer is also acting in some other capacity despite acting in the capacity of the service provider and is burdened with responsibilities in addition to which no special training is imparted to him in that regard.** On interrogation with some of the protection officers, it was found that they were not adequately trained and

almost all the protection officers in Assam were acting as the Director of Social Welfare Department reflecting that they were already acting in dual capacities. The Act provided appointment of protection officer for that purpose specifically. However, it was not implemented.

- **Ignorance was also the major cause of non-utilization of the Act.** It was seen in many places that people were ignorant of the legal provisions of the DV Act. Even the concept of zero FIR was not known to them. Moreover, it was found that in many cases even the advocates erred in filing cases under Section 498-A while they hardly advise the victim to make a complaint under the DV Act.
- **Shelter Homes not available in most of the places in India specially in the State of Assam, specifically for the victims of domestic violence.** Despite the direct and pinpointed provisions in the Act, there are no shelter homes and hence in this state of pandemic too the women prefer to suffer in silence as there are no ways out for women. Even the most educated and the renowned ladies are victims to domestic violence in this state of COVID-19.
- **Judicial Officer's opine that in most of the cases ex-parte decree is given which hardly comes to the rescue of the victim.** In most of the cases, it was found the victims are the worst sufferers and they could hardly get any relief as the abusers left the state or was altogether in a different state and hence he could easily go scot-free without providing adequate relief to the victim, for which even the law could hardly come to the rescue.
- **Victim's experience of hardship.** Marriage is a companionship and a feeling of security for the lady. But, when the feeling is itself threatened it makes no point in continuing the relation thereby causing mental trauma to oneself. Mostly, homemakers in rural areas are of the view that they are meant to suffer and the abusers, state of mind is that it is their right to torture their spouses.
- **Ignorance on the part of the victim and the family members regarding the notion of shared household.** It

should be noted that the victim is having the right to share the house and reside in the in-laws place even if it is not her husband's self acquired property. She cannot have an absolute right over the property but, can of course have a life time interest if her husband is residing in that property. The fact that, to seek protection under the Act, it need not be a self acquired property of her husband is a pertinent point which is unknown to many victims including the elder members of the family in which she is a resident.

- **Woman's education and autonomy.** While exploring the issue, many of the women suggested that violence was an important indicator of woman's autonomy and power within the household.

Conclusion

The research is suggestive of the fact that in present Indian scenario and setting, solutions to much of domestic violence must be found within the family setting and the community setting. The result of this study, though conducted within certain limitations gives a glimpse into both the severity and endemic nature of marital violence. The state's perspective and approach to domestic violence has the widest impact upon responses.

Suggestions

1. Modus operandi needs a transitional approach and the people need to play a pro-active role.
2. Non-governmental organizations needs to be nominated and shops or groceries in certain areas need to be well equipped.
3. India has to be human rights conscious and initiatives need to be taken to curb the menace. The Government could assign certain places and initiate policies by opening further websites in this regard.
4. The stakeholders should come out as service providers and caregivers and legal aid centres should come out as a rescue team and let it run round the clock so that the real scope of the Act could be mitigated.

5. The budding lawyers should take it as a mandated task and highlight the problems in National Commission for Women and the other concerned authorities. Collective public education imbibed with a sense of belongingness definitely has dynamic roles to play and create a just society imbibed with Constitutional morality.

   In the words of Pearl S. Buck, "Men and women should own the world as a mutual possession".

References

Bhattacharya, R. (2004). *Behind closed doors: Domestic Violence in India.* Panschsheel Enclave, New Delhi.

Bhandari, S., & Hughes C. (2017). "Lived Experiences of Women Facing Domestic Violence in India." *Journal of Social Work in the Global Community,* 14. Retrieved from https://scholarworks.waldenu.edu

Chhabra, S. (2018). "Effects of Societal Domestic Violence on health of Women", Retrieved from https://www.imedpub.com

Evans, M., Lindauer, M., Farell M. (2020). "A Pandemic within a pandemic—Intimate Partner Violence during COVID-19 Pandemic." *The New England Journal of Medicine.* Retrieved from https://www.nejm.org > doi>full

Hoseinnezhad, S., Elyasi, F., Shahhosseini Z. (2021). "A Rapid Review on Domestic Violence as a Silent Consequence in Corona Time: A Double Pandemic." *European Journal of Environment and Public Health.* Retrieved from https://www.ejeph.com>a-ra

Leela, V. (1999). "A summary report of Three Studies, September 1999—Domestic Violence In India." *Gujarat Institute of Development Studies.*

Metz, C. (2019). "Women Subjected to Domestic Violence: The impossibility of Separation." Retrieved from https://www.researchgate.net> files

Nigam, S. (2020). *Women and Domestic Violence Law in India.* Milton Park, Abingdon, New York.

Peterman, A., Potts, A., Thompson, K., Shah, N., Donell, M., (2020). "Pandemic and Violence against Women." *Centre for Global Studies.* Retrieved from https:///www.cgdev.org>files

Sweet, P. (2019). "Paradox of legibility: Domestic Violence and Institutional Survivorhood." Retrieved from https//academia.oup.com>

Yaw, A. & Mohammed, A. (2013). "Domestic Violence and its effect on Women." Retrieved from https://www.researchgate.net

12
Impact of COVID-19 on Social Inequalities and Gender

Asha B.N.

Introduction

It has now become that COVID-19 pandemic is not only a global health emergency, but it is also leading to major economic downturn and the COVID-19 pandemic is creating a strain on the economy and public health systems, it is also highlighting and magnifying, inequalities and the multiple forms of discrimination faced by women: the pandemic is moving beyond a global health crisis and changed into a labour market, social and economic crisis posing a serious threat to women's employment and livelihoods, especially in precarious informal and non-essential sectors.

The effects of the COVID-19 pandemic could reverse the limited progress that has been made on gender equality and women's rights. The corona virus outbreak aggravate existing inequalities for women across every sphere from health and the economy, to security and social protection, on this pandemic time women also play a disproportionate role in responding to the virus, including as frontline healthcare workers and carers at home, women's unpaid care work has increased significantly as school are closed. And the increased needs of older people, women are also harder hit by the economic impact of COVID-19 as they disproportionately work in insecure labour markets, nearly 60 per cent of women work in the informal economy and small industries, which puts them at greater risk of falling into poverty.

The Pandemic has also led to a steep increase in violence against women during lockdown with lockdown as many women are trapped at home with their abusers, facing domestic violence and are struggling to access helpline services. Since the outbreak of the pandemic, violence against women, particularly domestic violence has been increased. We can see that "The COVID-19 Pandemic is not only a health issue, it is a profound shock to our societies, economies and every sector of society, and women are working as frontline workers, health professionals. Community volunteers, transport and logistics managers, scientists and more, women are making critical contribution to address the outbreak every day."

Objectives of the study

1. Understand the gendered impacts of COVID-19 in the context of India.
2. To recommend effective policies and interventions as a means to be prepared and prevent the outbreak by cooperating women in the various processes.

Importance of the study

This chapter tries to raise awareness about some of the social inequalities and gender impacts that COVID-19 is having on our society. COVID-19 was intended to be ground-breaking for gender equality. Instead with the spread of COVID-19 pandemic even the limited gains made in the past decades are at risk of being rolled back. The COVID-19 pandemic is deepening pre-existing inequalities, increasing inequality in social, political and economic systems which are in turn amplifying the impacts of the pandemic. Across every sphere of life, from health to the economy, security to social protection, the impacts of COVID-19 are exacerbated for women and girls simply by virtue of their gender, this study can help to understand the effect of this pandemic crisis and recommend effective policies.

Sources of Data Used in Study

The data will be collected from secondary sources for this study. The secondary data will be collected from, research article and government orders, circulars, articles, newspapers.

The Effect of COVID-19 on Women

The COVID-19 is affecting women in many ways from concerns for their health and safety and income security to additional caring responsibilities and increased exposure to domestic violence, compounded economic impacts are felt especially by women who are generally earning less, saving less and holding insecure jobs or living close to poverty:

- Compounded economic impacts are effects especially on women who are generally earning very less, saving less and holding insecure jobs or living in poverty.
- Global value chains are being disrupted by COVID-19; women play a key role at every level as farmers, workers, processor entrepreneurs, buyers, service providers and employees.
- Women also working at the frontline as healthcare workers, working for long hours and exposing themselves to the risk while caring for patients yet their jobs are often the most undervalued and underpaid because of their gender.
- As a result of COVID-19 its effect on the health of women generally is adversely impacted through the reallocation of resources and priorities, including sexual and reproductive health services.
- Closure of school and childcare have placed significant additional care burdens on women in the home, it has put a spotlight on society's reliance on women's informal and formal care structures.
- The impact on other non-essential businesses, especially in the services sector, are particularly concerning for women as business owners and as employees, many of them are losing their livelihoods because working from home is not an option.
- As the COVID-19 pandemic increased economic and social stress, restricted movement and social isolation measures, gender based violence is increasing exponentially.

- Isolation and social distancing has increased the risk of domestic violence and abuse, women in violent relationships are not only exposed to their abuser for long periods of time, and they are unable to leave home or discreetly call helpline.
- Women tend to rely much more on public transport than men, putting women at greater risk of catching COVID-19 as they commute to work, care for relatives or do grocery shopping.
- Social distancing is not possible for everyone; millions of householders depend on daily care and help from women as primary caretakers.

Further we can see that the Economic and Social impacts on all are severe. They are more so for women, many of the industries in the formal economy directly affected by quarantines and lockdown, travel tourism, restaurants, food production have very high female labour force participation, women also constitute a large percentage of the informal economy in informal markets and agriculture around the world, in both developed and developing economies, many informal sector jobs domestic workers, caregivers are mostly done by women who typically lack health insurance and have no social safety net to fall back. At the same time, women typically shoulder a greater burden of taking care on average women did three times as much unpaid care work as men at home even before COVID-19. Now formal sector female employees with children are balancing one or more of the following: work, childcare, homeschooling, elder care, and house work, female headed households are particularly vulnerable.

The crisis is directly affecting on women's health and safety. Apart from the impacts of the disease, women may find it hard to access much needed maternal health services given that all services are being directed to essential medical needs availability of contraception and service for other needs may become disrupted. Women's health safety is also in risk, so they needed to battle with the disease, isolation, social distancing, restrictions on freedom of movement are, perversely, the very conditions that feed into the hands of abusers who now find state-sanctioned circumcising abuse.

Women are also working as frontline workers and nurses, their risk of infection is higher, so while attention must be paid to ensuring safe conditions for all caregivers, special attention is needed for female nurses and carers not only in access to personal protective equipments like masks but also for other needs such as menstrual hygiene product essential to ensuring they are able to function well.

It is shocking how many of the key decision makers in the process of designing and executing the pandemic responses are men. This is not surprising, that women still do not enjoy the same level of participation in major decision making bodies: governments, parliaments, cabinets or corporations as men do, only some per cent of parliamentarians worldwide are women, and less than 10 per cent of heads of state or government are women. While we have a few shining examples of women heads of government, women are conspicuous by their absence in decision making for in this pandemic.

Here are Some Actions Government Need to Take

1. Government needs to ensure the female nurses and doctors are integrated into every aspect of the response effort, ensuring the menstrual hygiene products and tampons are available for female caregivers and frontline responders as part of personal protective equipment, this will ensure that they do not face unnecessary discomforts in already challenging situations, support in terms of much needed critical medical equipment.
2. Ensure the services for all victims of domestic abuse are considered 'essential services' and are kept open and law enforcement is sensitized to the need to be responsive to calls from victims, shelters for women survivors in the list of essential services, this will ensure that the pandemic does not inadvertently lead to more trauma, injury and deaths during the quarantine period given the high proportion of violent death of women perpetrated by intimate partners.
3. Social protection measures that reflect an understanding of women's special circumstances and for those most in need and paid and, or sick leave for those who are unable

to come to work because they are taking care of children or elders at home. For informal sector employees, who constitute the vast majority of the female labour force in developing economies, special efforts should be made to deliver compensatory payments. Identifying those informal sector workers will be a challenge and will need to take account of a country's particular circumstance, but it is worth the effort to ensure more equity in outcomes.

4. They have to include women in political participation, in response and recovery decision making, whether at the local, municipal or national level, bringing the voices of women into decision making it lead to better outcomes, policy makers should leverage the capacities of women's organization. Reaching out to enlist women's groups will help ensure a more robust community response as their considerable network can be leveraged to disseminate and amplify social distancing.
5. Policy makers must pay attention to what is happening in people's homes and support an equal sharing of the burden of care between women and men there is a great opportunity to 'Unstereotype' the gender roles that play out in households in many parts of the world, one concrete action for governments, particularly for male leaders, is to join our campaign, He For She and stay tuned for more information about 'He For She @home', where by we enlistment and boys to ensure that they are doing their fair share at home and alleviating some of the care burdens that fall disproportionately on women.

These actions will lead in building the needs of women and offers an opportunity to implement policy actions that build a more social equality.

Conclusion

The COVID-19 pandemic is affecting all countries, destroying jobs, increasing poverty, and putting risk in gender equality gains, policy makers around the world are rightly focusing on responding to the immediate crisis fighting the devastating effects of the pandemic on healthcare systems whilst trying to keep their economies alive, the next step to find the tools to sustain economic growth, fight poverty, and regain the lost ground in gender equality–gender responsive fiscal policies are a viable answer can magnify the effect of the crisis, across several social, economic and political dimension.

References

Asadullah, M. Niaz and Raghunathan Kalyani, (June 25, 2020). "Fighting Gender Inequality in India During the COVID-19 Pandemic." *The Diplomat*, https://thediplomat.com/2020/06/fighting-gender-inequality-in-india

COVID-19 and Gender Equality, (2020). https://eige,europe.eu/topics/health/covid- 19 and - gender equality.

Dutt Pankhuri and Prasad Urvashi, (April 18, 2020). "Understanding Inequality and COVID-19 Pandemic." ET Government, https://www.google.com/amp/s/government.economictimes.indiatimes.com/amp/news/healthcare/understanding-inequality-and-covid-19-pandamic/75216392

EIGE, (2020). COVID-19 and gender equality, https://eige.europe.eu/topics/health/covid-19-and-gender-equality.

Human Development Reports, (2020). Gender Inequality and the COVID-19 crisis: A Human Development Programme.

World Bank Group, (April 16, 2020). Gender dimensions of the COVID-19 Pandemic Policy Note.

UN Women Deputy Executive Director Anita Bhartia, (March 26, 2020). *Women and COVID-19: Five Things Governments can do Now.*

Shah Kadambari, (May 17, 2020), "How COVID-19 is amplifying Gender Inequality in India." *The Indian Express.*

13
COVID-19 and Labour Migration: Challenges for Business Sectors in India

Kasturi Bora and *Bhaswati Borah*

Introduction

Migration is the movement of people away from their usual place of residence, across either internal (within the country) or international (across countries) borders. India has been under lockdown since March 25, 2020. During this time, activities not contributing to the production and supply of essential goods and services were completely or partially suspended. Passenger trains and flights were halted. The lockdown has severely impacted migrants, several of whom lost their jobs due to shutting of industries and were stranded outside their native places wanting to get back. Since then, the government has announced relief measures for migrants and made arrangements for migrants to return to their native places. The Supreme Court of India, recognising the problems faced by migrants stranded in different parts of the country, reviewed transportation and relief arrangements made by the government. On June 9, 2020, the Court directed Central and State Governments to complete transportation of remaining stranded migrants and expand the focus of relief measures to facilitate employment for returning migrants.

Indian migrant workers during the COVID-19 pandemic have faced multiple hardships. With factories and workplaces shut down due to the lockdown imposed in the country, millions of migrant workers had to deal with the loss of income, food shortages and uncertainty about their future. Following this, many of them and their families went hungry. Thousands of them then began walking back home, with no means of transport due to the lockdown. In response, the Central and State Governments took various measures to help them, and later arranged transport for them. More than 300 migrant workers died due to the lockdown, with reasons ranging from starvation, suicides, exhaustion, road and rail accidents, police brutality and denial of timely medical care.

Migrant workers who decided to stay back during the exodus faced assault from their neighbours, who accused them of being infected with corona virus. They thus could not venture out to buy food. Many also faced police brutality if they ventured out of their homes. Upon their return to their hometowns and villages, they were treated with either fear or a "class bias", being hosed down with disinfectants or soap solution in some cases. They were feared to be carrying corona virus from the urban areas where they had been employed. They faced assault and harassment from the people of their hometowns. Since many of them belonged to the lower castes, they had to face caste slurs. Thousands got into property disputes. Migrants travelling by Shramik Special trains reported that food and water provisions were either not provided or simply dumped at the entrances of the trains, leaving workers fighting with each other to get their share. Passengers then hurriedly filled their water bottles at the railway stations that the trains stopped at. Many migrant workers expressed a fear of returning to their old jobs in the cities, after facing unemployment during the lockdown. Companies reported labour shortages from mid-April.

Despite government promises and schemes to generate employment in rural areas, some migrant workers began going back to the cities due to lack of employment in their hometowns, as lockdown restrictions were reduced as part of Unlock 1.0 in June. A large number of these were returning to Mumbai. The reopening of the regular services of the railways also helped facilitate this. The cities, too, reported major shortages of labour, especially in the construction industry. A study conducted in April-May stated that 77 per cent migrant workers were prepared to return to cities for work. The return of the migrants to cities is expected to help revive the economy, which had sustained an impact. Some employers sponsored the travel of migrants back to their workplaces. This included taxis, trains and even flights.

Indian Migrant Workers during the COVID-19 Pandemic

There are an estimated 139 million migrants in the country, according to the World Economic Forum. The International Labour Organization (ILO) predicted that due to the pandemic and the lockdown, about 400 million workers would be poverty-stricken. Most migrants in the country originate from Uttar Pradesh and Bihar, followed by Rajasthan and Madhya Pradesh. The cities of Mumbai and Delhi attract the highest number of migrants. While most men migrate for work, women migrate due to marriage.

Migrant workers majorly comprise of daily-wage labourers working in the manufacturing and construction industries. They are often denied adequate healthcare, nutrition, housing and sanitation, since many of them work in the informal sector. They are mostly from rural areas but live in cities for work for most of the year. Many have no savings and lived in factory dormitories, which were shut due to the lockdown. Additionally, there was no central registry of migrant workers, despite the existence of the Inter-State Migrant Workmen Act, 1979.

According to research published in the Royal Geographical Society, the workers who have been treated the worst are from areas like Odisha, Jharkhand and Chhattisgarh, in which the indigenous population's natural resources were extracted by outsiders. Further, workers paid the least for the hardest work belong to the backward classes, mainly from the *Dalit* and the *Adivasi* communities. The research also indicated that the families of the migrant workers supported them by maintaining their houses and taking care of them, either when seasonal work is unavailable or when they are no longer able to work. Maharashtra has the largest number of migrants, according to the 2011 Census of India. Its state government imposed a lockdown on 20 March in Pune, Pimpri-Chinchwad, the Mumbai Metropolitan Region and Nagpur, leaving the migrant workers with no work. Thousands then gathered at the train termini and bus stations, seeking transport to their hometowns. With the nationwide lockdown, all transport facilities were closed.

Challenges Faced by Power and Renewable Energy Sectors in India Due to COVID-19 and Labour Migration

The COVID-19 pandemic has pushed the country under an extended lockdown creating a cascading effect on economic growth but the labour migration caused by it is posing serious challenges for the power and renewable energy industries. The exodus of migrant labourers from major metro cities has given rise to a shortage of non-technical workers working in the energy industry and even if the government opts for a staggered lifting of the lockdown, the process of remobilisation would pose challenges for companies, according to industry executives.

"Demobilisation of labour is still easy but remobilisation is not. Bringing people from Uttar Pradesh and Bihar in this current environment will be difficult. So, we will have major challenges in manufacturing operations which currently have been completely shut. I think even after this lockdown, the disruption to the business will be there", said Ashish Khanna, MD & CEO, Tata Power Solar and President, Tata Power Renewables. He added that if there is a possibility of a staggered release, the firm will not be able to upscale 200 to 1,200 employees in a two-month time, which is an original project schedule.

Also, Tata Power's Managing Director and Chief Executive Officer (CEO), Praveer Sinha, said that as of now the company is doing fine and is fully supported by the contractual workforce but most renewable operation and maintenance (O&M) projects and thermal power projects need extended workforce and the concerns remain across the sectors.

According to Ranjit Gupta, Chief Executive Officer at Azure Power, deployment of labour will be a huge challenge given the restrictions on intra and interstate public transportation. *"There has been huge migration of labour in the last few weeks and with limited intra and interstate public transport available, they may find it difficult to return to the work sites which could cause further delays, we are looking for the government to respond allowing our labour to safely to return to work"*, he said.

All the under-construction renewable energy projects are likely to receive due extensions on the grounds of national lockdown of about one-and-a-half months – March 25, 2020 to May 3, 2020 and remobilisation of labour, according to Amod Khanorkar, Senior Director at ratings agency Care Ratings.

The Ministry of New and Renewable Energy has already announced an informal clarification mentioning the duration of the lockdown and the time required to remobilise the workforce should be taken into consideration while granting the extension.

The supply and labour disruptions from the current lockdown could delay project execution in financial year 2020-21 till the time migrant labourers resume work, Care Ratings said in a recent report. It, however, added that though the spread of corona virus has impacted the availability of workforce, limited O&M staff is allowed to work on specific permissions.

Khanorkar said that for operational projects, labour intensity is low but for under-implementation projects it is high, as they require usage of unskilled labour to a large extent.

According to Manish Gupta, Senior Director, Crisil Ratings, for under-construction solar projects technical requirements are high at an advanced stage hence, labour intensity is lower. *"In case of operational projects, both technical and local manpower is required and as most of the utility-scale projects are in hinterlands where local labour is used so mobility issues will not impact much"*, Gupta said. But, if we compare the impact of the migration challenge between the wind and solar sector, the impact would be less on wind, according to sector analysts. *"The impact would be less because, one, the number of projects under construction in solar is higher than wind and, two, the relative intensity of EPC work is lower in wind"*, said Gupta. According to Khanorkar, wind power generation during March and April as it is very low so lower O&M would have a very marginal impact.

India's renewable energy target of 175 GW by 2022 had the potential to create employment for over 3,30,000 workers in the wind and solar sectors – at least 2,30,000 additional workers between 2019 and 2022, according to a report by the Council on Energy, Environment and Water, the Natural Resources Defense Council, and the Skill Council for Green Jobs released last year.

Rapid capacity addition in India's solar and wind sectors have been the primary drivers behind the growth. It added that in 2019, nearly 1,00,000 workers were employed in the solar and wind industry. While it is difficult to predict the overall impact of labour migration on renewable energy jobs, Gupta said that looking at the current situation, job creation would continue to happen in the renewable sector.

"The tendering activity for renewable capacities has continued unabated and since January this year, the amount of capacity that has been tendered out is the same as that last year. So, there is a good pace of awarding activities that is happening and this COVID-19 issue is short term. At this point, I think job creation will continue to happen in the renewable sector", Gupta added.

He said in order to tackle this issue on a short-term basis, the government should defer the commissioning dates for completion of under-construction projects as they have defined timelines given by their project authorities.

Concerns have also been flagged by the emerging start-ups in the electric vehicle (EV) industry. Nishchal Chaudhary, founder and CEO of Jaipur-based EV start-up BattRE said that the industry will have to grapple with multiple challenges to come back on track once the lockdown is over.

"Some of the key parts of the supply chain will be affected and it might take two to three months for it to stabilise after lockdown. In the case of many companies, the factory employees are migrants from other states, it is going to be challenging to reach the full production capacities, as many of the employees will choose not to resume work immediately after lockdown", said Chaudhary.

According to the National Electricity Plan released in 2018, for the capacity addition of considered 1,76,140 megawatt (MW) including renewables of 1,17,756 MW and 48,261 MW of thermal power plants under construction in the period 2017-22, the additional manpower requirement shall be of the order of 253.76 thousands out of which 194.91 thousands will be technical and 58.85 thousands will be non-technical.

Challenges Faced by Few More Sectors in India Due to COVID-19 and Labour Migration

Entrepreneurs and exporters are struggling to crank up operations just when the government has relaxed stern restrictions, because labourers have imposed a virtual lockdown by returning home in droves. Apart from labourers anxious to return home after over a month of rough, jobless existence, businesses are also being squeezed by problems of logistics and transportation and financial hardships owing to the lockdown. Industry leaders said April-June quarter would be a washout even for the high and mighty, but would be catastrophic for SMEs.

"We will have to deal with it by incentivising workers at least for sites that need urgent attention due to onset of monsoon. Hopefully, supply of raw material will smoothen out soon", said Jaxay Shah, national chairman of CREDAI.

Projects may miss deadlines. *"As the supply chain for construction materials is expected to be normalised in the next few weeks, insufficient labour strength could severely impact the construction operations in the weeks to come"*, said a spokesperson for Shapoorji Pallonji Engineering & Construction.

Biscuits and Bottled Water

George Angelo, chief executive of Bisleri, said reverse migration will create shortage of trained labour in industrial centres and put stress on logistics and local distribution. *"It will increase the labour costs and impact operating efficiencies in the medium term."* He said migrants faced extreme hardship. *"Thousands have become skeptical of their future, and combined with the looming fear of exposure to the pandemic, are returning to their villages."*

"The lack of migrant labour does pose a problem, but we are hopeful that going forward, local labour will make up for the absence of the migrants", Parle Products category head Mayank Shah said.

Mobile Phones

The India Cellular & Electronics Association expects 30 per cent normalcy by the end of May. *"Departure of labour to their home towns should be avoided by motivating them"*, said Chairman, Pankaj Mohindroo.

But even 30 per cent normalcy seems difficult. Foxconn has got approval to resume production with 10 per cent workforce, but getting labour is turning out to be a big challenge, said a source.

Manpower was a "herculean task", said Manu Jain, Xiaomi India head. *"We have manpower, yes; sufficient, no ... It will take a few weeks to sort it out"*, he said.

Small & Medium Units

Anil Bhardwaj, Secretary General of the Federation of Indian Micro and Small & Medium Enterprises, said workers won't return soon because of welfare schemes. *"They will not want to come back to cities anytime soon, unless they were making a lot of money"*, he said, adding that small businesses would resume with 20-25 per cent activity.

Mukesh Mohan Gupta, President of the Chamber of Indian MSMEs, said small businesses were still facing issues pertaining to social distancing, sanitisation and difficulty in finding labour. *"For the labour still present in the cities, lack of public transport is a deterrent for movement to factories ... Many businesses are reluctant to start because of fear of inspection by district authorities and subsequent sealing of facilities if things are not found in order"*, Gupta said.

Food Processing and Agri Exports

"Supply of jams, sauces, juices and purees could be in short supply due to labour shortage and difficulty in getting working capital loans at low interest rates. Retail shelves may dry up soon as manufacturers have stock for only 3-4 weeks", said Subodh Jindal, President of All India Food Processors' Association.

Shipments of bulk agricultural commodities from India are choked by labour scarcity at ports. Many migrant workers at big ports in Mundra, Kandla and Nhava Sheva want to return home. *"In two days, around 10,000 workers engaged at Kandla had registered to return to native states. The reverse migration would halt global shipments for several months"*, said Tushar Anam, Chairman of V Arjoon Shipping Private Ltd. He said daily dispatches had revived to 30-40 containers from the usual 200-250 containers in the past few weeks.

"Most workers are unlikely to return for the next three months once they reach home. Local leaders in Uttar Pradesh, Bihar and Rajasthan need to appeal to the workers to stay put in their places of work", said Devendra Shah, MD of Liladhar Pasoo Freight, based in Mumbai. He said the Container Freight Association of India has written to the Centre to prevent reverse migration of workers.

Small Business Solutions for Pandemic Challenges

The COVID-19 pandemic is hurting small enterprises globally. But socio-economic pressures are particularly severe in developing countries, where resources are limited and economic activity weak and small business frequently the backbone of growth. The pandemic threatens to throw economies into recession and push tens of millions of households back or even deeper into poverty. The pandemic's impact will be disproportionate in least-developed and small-island developing countries, notably in Africa and in the Pacific, which are especially vulnerable to economic volatility and shocks. Their health systems and economies are less able to cope with challenges, leaving their poor and vulnerable groups at increased risk.

Exogenous trade shocks are transmitted through the global value chain. Large retailers have closed stores, hurting factories and workers locked into just-in-time supply chains in countries including Bangladesh and Cambodia. Many micros, small and medium-sized enterprises are fighting for survival as a result. Yet they must cover salaries, rent, and other operating expenses, debts to financial institutions, and taxes.

Many will see letting go of workers as the best solution. This could transform economic crisis into social calamity. Fortunately, the focus of most businesses for now is on protecting employees, understanding the risks to their business, and in managing supply chain disruptions. This will be important for safeguarding jobs and incomes, preserving financial stability, and to revive growth by minimizing disruptions to trade and global supply chains. Quick recovery of these businesses can mitigate the most dire consequences. But beyond the immediate recovery, we need to ensure the medium to long-term survival of small businesses by removing impediments to their growth.

The key challenges will be to improve access to finance and investment for small enterprises, give them more freedom to expand into new sectors, and promote their use of new technologies to better connect with producers, suppliers and consumers.

The first challenge is the biggest. Banks are often reluctant to lend due to a lack of market information, concerns about risk, and poor quality loan applications. Unless investors, entrepreneurs, and viable businesses can be financed, opportunities will be wasted and growth potential squandered. Business laws and regulations can be overhauled to suit the needs of modern commerce. In many countries, starting a business involves high costs and long delays, compromising investment and business growth. This is a key reason behind the large informal labour markets of some countries. Efforts must be made to remove bureaucratic red tape to allow businesses to open and operate as quickly as possible when COVID-19 restrictions are eased.

A second step is to rethink the role of state-owned enterprises to provide extra space for small enterprises to grow. In many countries, state-owned enterprises provide essential services such as power generation, water, sewage, and telecommunications. But they can be inefficient, drain government resources, and generate low returns. Many are monopolies. The pandemic might provide governments with opportunities to allow micro, small and medium-sized enterprises to provide some of these essential services.

In tandem, competition and consumer protection frameworks can be improved, especially in markets where participation of governments may be extensive and a few firms dominate key sectors. This reduces consumer choices, keeps prices high, and constrains small businesses. Better consumer protections would reduce the scope for price controls and gouging, which distorts markets and impacts heavily on consumers.

A priority is also to give women the tools to realize their potential to run businesses, broadening avenues to contribute to community welfare and economic growth. Female-led businesses can be encouraged through training in business processes, access to finance, and addressing customary practices that favour men over women. To promote female entrepreneurs in Armenia, for example, such programmes resulted in more business registrations by women, improved skills, and better access to finance, while financial institutions were guided on hiring more female loan officers. Finally, small businesses can be supported to reinvent their business models using new technologies.

A potentially promising sector is healthcare, currently a global priority as the world battles COVID-19. Instead of having to travel to the nearest major city to see a specialist, tele-health platforms provide virtual diagnosis, treatment, preventive and curative services, as well as training for health care professionals in areas such as epidemiology and pandemic influenza risk communication. These services are becoming indispensable and seem tailor-made for micro, small and medium-sized enterprises with sufficient expertise and capital.

Support for the agriculture sector innovations can provide further fertile ground for these businesses. Already, small-scale farmers are using innovative technologies and practices to raise yields, manage inputs more efficiently, introduce new crops and production systems, and enhance product quality. With well-targeted support, such practices can be crucial to business survival in the current crisis. For instance, governments can invest in satellite-based earth observation technology to provide smallholder farmers with continuous data on land and water resources. Satellite information on water levels and weather forecasts can help smallholder farmers reduce water stress and consumption while raising yields by as much as 200–250 per cent. Tailoring these approaches to specific country circumstances could help save millions of livelihoods in poor communities and fortify economies against future shocks.

Conclusion

It is important to plan how to deal with the economic fallout and rebuild a more inclusive economy in a post-COVID-19 world, and much of that hinges on how we revive labour markets and livelihoods crises highlight the chasms in a society. This crisis is deepening ours. For long, India has hidden behind the guise of diversity to conceal socially sanctioned discrimination on the basis of caste, religion, and gender. Discrimination that has manifested in deep socio-economic disparities that are now important determinants of how equipped people are to weather the current storm. The COVID-19 pandemic and the ensuing lockdown have not only cast a spotlight on how vulnerable such a large share of India's population is, but also how much more vulnerable it is when compared with others. It is imperative that the government continue to institute, and expand, immediate relief measures for the disadvantaged. But equally important is the pressing need to start planning for how to deal with the economic fallout and rebuild a more inclusive economy in a post-COVID-19 world. Much of this hinges on how we revive labour markets and livelihoods.

The current picture is bleak. The travel ban and lockdown have induced a slump in nearly all sectors of the economy—from manufacturing and construction to retail trade, hotels and restaurants, as well as agriculture. Not only does this affect workers directly employed in these sectors, but also the many vendors that are indirectly connected. Finding themselves suddenly out of work, unable to pay rent or to feed themselves, hundreds of thousands of migrants and daily-wage labourers made a desperate attempt to go back from cities to their hometowns; some finding themselves rounded up in vain by authorities to be placed in makeshift shelters.

The ensuing severe labour shortage is disrupting agriculture and supply chains. Bottlenecks in obtaining e-passes and police aggression towards those leaving their homes, truckers abandoning their loads, a lack of workers for production, loading and unloading of vehicles, are further crippling the economy. Employers are struggling to make payroll, either because they cannot physically deliver the payments to their workers and they are not set up to make electronic transfers, or because the slump in business means they don't have the funds. Many informal and formal micro and small businesses will inevitably fold. Most self-employed workers – many of them survivalist micro-entrepreneurs, hawkers and small vendors, domestic helps, or gig workers – have lost their incomes because they are locked in their homes and/or have seen demand dry up. Working remotely is not an option for the socio-economically disadvantaged relying on physical labour and the provision of location-based services for income. The travel ban and lockdown may be temporary but their effects will be long-term. The loss of Rs. 10,000 crore in taxes for every day of the lockdown comes at a time when the government's historically small spending on health infrastructure has to rise to combat the pandemic, and emergency bailouts need to be financed.

In order to dig out our way from the crisis, first, an economic crisis such as this transforms the fiscal calculus. The government must loosen its fiscal restraint to help the economy stabilise, recover, and grow.

Second, businesses need funding to tide over the crisis. Not only should there be a moratorium on loans, but the government also needs to ensure the provision of working capital at low interest rates to start-ups, and small and medium businesses. The effect on bank capitalisation needs to be factored in. Once the pandemic is under control, the government must foster investments in infrastructure – this is one of the fastest and most direct way to create jobs.

Third, reducing the tax compliance burden is critical; especially for small businesses, this is a good time to simplify payments and expand the net, even if no additional revenue is expected at this time.

Fourth, governments can support businesses by providing

wage subsidies directly to workers through digital payments. This will ensure that the workforce is recorded and registered, enabling the government to reach out to them, now and in the future. It will assist businesses to retain workers at a time of stressed cash flow.

Fifth, the government must enable universal access to social safety nets, including healthcare, maternity, disability and pension benefits for all workers. Crises like this one not only underscore the need for healthcare, but such benefits can also help smooth consumption during times of distress and demand shocks.

Sixth, the harmonisation of the labyrinth of labour laws into four codes has gone some ways in clearing out the regulatory logjams that have plagued us for many years, but the rules for the codes have yet to be defined. Investors value certainty greatly. Leaving our labour codes vague undermines one the objectives – a clear, consistent and implementable labour code is good for business and investment as well as for workers.

Finally, despite a deepening deficit, we cannot lose sight of the fact that our education and skill training systems are in desperate need of an overhaul. These will demand greater funds, but the first priority must be to improve access to good-quality education for children who are losing out right now. Children are not in school during the lockdown. While the middle- and upper-class have access to distance learning, those from disadvantaged households do not. So, this sets the children from disadvantaged backgrounds even further behind in their trajectories.

Chinese strategist, Sun-Tzu noted that *"In the midst of chaos, there is also opportunity"*. Then for us, the opportunity to set India on a more inclusive path abounds.

References

https://en.wikipedia.org/wiki/Indian_migrant_workers_during_the_COVID-19_pandemic#:~:text=Many%20migrant%20workers%20expressed%20a,at%20least%20another%20six%20months.

https://thelogicalindian.com/story-feed/awareness/understanding-impact-of-lockdown-on-migrants-in-india-21669

https://economictimes.indiatimes.com/news/company/corporate-trends/after-being-locked-down-cos-now-set-to-suffer-labour-pain/articleshow/75542263.cms?from=mdr

https://www.itcilo.org/stories/labour-migration-time-covid-19

https://blogs.adb.org/small-business-solutions-for-pandemic-challenges

14

Poverty and the Pandemic: A Quantitative Impact Analysis of Urban Settlements in India

Lovepreet Singh, Tanmoyee Bhattacharjee and *Anjali Thakur*

Introduction

Lack of employment avenues in the rural areas has resulted in large-scale unplanned migration of masses to urban settlements. This has resulted in the low wage earners to live in unhygienic and deprived conditions due to highly segregated urban development because of underlying economic and social reasons. Amidst the rising demand for employment and the skewed corresponding growth in employment opportunities, the migrant workers lacking the required education and skill training seek out work in cities' informal economy. Due to lack of affordable urban housing, the workers find spaces wherever they can to settle and form communities as more people join. Such settlements are characterised by overcrowding, unsanitary and unwary environment, lack of drinking water and basic healthcare, poor quality of life as the authorities and public utilities can only serve those registered on paper. All these factors combined play a significant role in perpetuating poverty in urban settlements.

The outbreak of COVID-19 and the absence of job security left such migrant workers exasperated and fearful of the uncertain future that they and their families had ahead of them. After the imposition of nationwide lockdown on 24th March, 2020, while the citizens embraced social distancing norms and focused on keeping themselves safe at home, a large strata of the population did not have the privilege to do so. Rather, more than catching the disease, making the two ends meet and feeding their families was the primary concern. As the population living in marginalised urban settlements primarily comprises of domestic workers, daily wage earners and street vendors, they lack job security and any economic safety net.

To understand the impact of COVID on such marginalised communities, a team from Shakti Shalini, an organisation that supports survivors of gender/sexual violence across India, conducted an impact study considering a sample of 120 households residing in five socio-economically marginalised communities of south-east Delhi in September 2020. The survey primarily catered to facets pertaining to economic condition/employment, availability of food, and lack of access to regular classrooms/education on individuals of the communities. These three areas were identified with regard to which the tool of data collection was prepared. The survey also seeks to plan the future course of action for facilitating assistance concerning the identified areas of interventions. The survey research was conducted in the south-east district of Delhi in the following communities: Nehru Nagar Block 7, Block 10, Aadiwasi Camp, Jal Vihar, and Sriniwaspuri. These communities consist of people who have migrated from rural areas to urban settlements for better employment and living conditions. The majority of the population from these communities, especially men, work as daily wage earners, *dholwalas,* perform puppet shows, make toys, taxi drivers and sell home-made herbal products, whereas women either assist their partners in household chores or work as domestic workers in the neighbourhood. They are largely Hindu communities of mixed castes; a few sections include Muslim communities and tribal folks. Health, hygiene, employment, and educational standards are poor; basic amenities of water, electricity, drainage, public toilets may vary in accessibility and quality from one community to the other, and certain communities live in temporary sheds and shelters. Gender and sexual violence and discrimination in education, healthcare, domestic work are common; domestic violence, public harassment, forced/early and child marriages are frequent. Rampant alcoholism and drug use and abuse enhance masculine violence; women and children live in extreme vulnerability within the communities.

Objectives

(a) To identify specific challenges faced by marginalized communities with regard to education, employment, and ration amidst the pandemic.

(b) To gather information in order to plan the future course of action for facilitating assistance.

Methodology

Research Design

The descriptive and co-relational research design was employed because the survey aims to describe a certain phenomenon using quantifiable descriptors and co-relational because it seeks to find a significant relationship between identified variables.

Sample Size and Sample Selection

120 households were considered for the study, selected through purposive sampling technique under non-probability sampling. As these communities were urban slums consists of a pool of migrant workers and daily wage with severe livelihood implications due to the outbreak of the pandemic. Further, 24 respondents from each community were selected by using random sampling under probability sampling for equal representation and unbiased statistics.

Methods and Tools of Data Collection

The team collected the data through a well-defined set of questions, developed after detailed primary study. Following the social distancing norms, the trained enumerators collected the data via phone calls. A structured close-ended questionnaire was designed as a tool to collect data. The questionnaire consisted of questions pertaining to education, food security (ration), and employment.

Data Processing and Analysis

The data collected from 120 respondents were statistically analysed, the findings of which are shown with the help of tables and charts.

Table 14.1: Personal profile of the respondents

AGE	NUMBER (FREQUENCY)	PERCENTAGE (%)
16-24	36	30
25-33	41	34.16
34-42	33	27.5
43-51	7	5.83
52-60	3	2.5
GENDER		
MALE	42	35
FEMALE	78	65
EDUCATION		
NOT LITERATE	50	41.66
PRIMARY	24	20
SECONDARY	21	17.5
Sr. SECONDARY	16	13.33
COLLEGE/UNIVERSITY	9	7.5
HOUSING		
OWN	62	51.66
RENT	58	48.33
CHILDREN		
GIRLS	18	15
BOYS	11	9.16
BOTH	74	61.66
NONE	17	14.16
FAMILY MEMBERS		
2-6	94	78.33
7-11	26	21.66

From the above data it can be seen that majority of the respondents were female belonging from the age group of 25-33 followed by 16-24 and 34-42 respectively. 41.66 per cent of the respondents did not have any formal education whereas 20 per cent and 17.5 per cent had completed their primary and secondary level education respectively. Only 13.33 per cent and 7.5 per cent consisted of residents who had completed senior secondary level and went to college respectively. A very minimal difference has been seen with regard to the housing of the respondents. 51.66 per cent of the respondents were having their own *jhuggis* (slum housing) whereas 48.33 per cent were staying on rent. Majority of our respondents had both girl and boy child in their family amounting to 61.66 per cent, 15 per cent of the families had only girl child, 9.16 per cent of families had only boy child and 14.16

per cent of the families had no child. 78.33 per cent of the families who participated in this survey had 2-6 members in their family whereas the other 21.66 per cent of the families had 7-11 members in each family.

Literature Review

In the paper (Laxman, Manjula, 2020) refers to Credit Suisse Global Wealth Report (2017) to stress upon the inequality among the Indian population. The report shows top 10 per cent of the households held 52.9 per cent of the total wealth of the country in 2002 which increased to 62.1 per cent by 2012 stating that India is among the most unequal countries in the world. According to (ILO, Ralf Hussmanns, 2004) informal employment is defined by lack of a work book, lack of social security system, lack of entitlement to paid annual or sick leaves, lack of a written employment contract or the casual/temporary nature of work.

When we talk about marginalised urban settlements we are mostly talking about daily wage labourers, domestic workers and migrant labourers who in big cities are engaged in the above defined informal employment. Thus, one can only imagine how vulnerable the socially and economically marginalised sections would be in a nationwide lockdown as the uncertainty hit them with regards to their wage income which in turn affects all other sections of their lives like education, food security and health.

Justifying the above mentioned statement with a substantial fact from (Dev & Sengupta, 2020) paper which stated that out of total employment accounting for 465 million workers, 422 million (90.7%) were informal workers in 2017-18 making India score highest share of informal employment.

(Mehrotra & Parida, 2019) in their paper highlights a representation of informal employment from 2004-05, 2011-12 to 2017-18:

Year	Total Employment (in millions)	Informal Employment (in millions)	% share of informal workers in total employment
2004-05	459.4	430.9	93.8
2011-12	474.2	436.6	92.5
2017-18	465.1	421.9	90.7

As shown in the table almost 90 per cent accounts for informal workers, though the table shows a decreasing trend but now given the pandemic situation with the nation going through several lockdowns the given percentage is enough to push major strata to extreme poverty.

Laxman, Manjula (2020) in her paper shows how the intensity of the COVID-19 crisis followed by the nationwide lockdown made the people living in urban settlements, called slums, adjusted to the wage loss and lack of income from cutting down their expenditure on their social life, health and education to cutting down their expenditure on even absolute necessities (food, shelter, clothing). It further came down to reducing even the quantity of food intake.

(Daniel, Gerszon et al., 2020) in their paper mention that India scores the highest among the 42 million of population in South Asia who will be pushed in extreme poverty.

With the already wider gap in between rich and poor in India and economic disparity, the COVID-19 pandemic situation cropped up as a phenomenon which would further marginalise the already socially and economically marginalised communities who were just trying to hold the grip but the pandemic pushing them to where they started from or even worse.

Survey Findings

Ration

48 per cent of the total 120 households surveyed did not have a ration card. 65 per cent (78) of the surveyed families reported to have faced difficulty in procuring ration during the pandemic whereas 53 per cent (63) of the families had a ration card. These families (65%) procured ration through various mediums—ration drives conducted by NGOs (51%), various individuals (22%), government initiatives (15%), and 12% managed procuring ration through other mediums.

As reported by the respondents, 59 per cent of the surveyed families experienced shortage of ration because of reasons such as inadequate supply (51%), large families (40%), and poor quality of ration (9%). Due to the insufficiency of ration provisions, 53 per cent of the families reported to had rationalise and cut down on their food consumption.

Despite an ease in the government-imposed lockdown due to COVID, 71 per cent families reported shortage of ration in August 2020 because of cascading effect of the lockdown. Major reason for lack of ration after the lockdown is loss of employment, deduction in salary and wages. The data shows that 60 per cent of the families reported difficulty in finding work, 32 per cent reported working for lower/inadequate compensation for work, rendering them with lesser disposable income, 8 per cent reported other reasons affecting access and sufficiency of ration provisions. 35 per cent of the respondents reported that the uncertainty around making the ends meet harmfully affected their physical and mental health, among these, 61 per cent respondents experienced physical weakness, 35 per cent had to consult a doctor or visit a hospital for deteriorating health and 4 per cent of the respondents reported to have experienced stress, anxiety and other health issues.

Employment

The members of the communities primarily rely on unorganised sector for employment. The data shows that 58 per cent families are dependent upon a single earning member and amongst those who are employed, 29 per cent of the respondents work as domestic help, 19 per cent own small businesses and shops,17 per cent constitute migrant labourers and 12 per cent of the respondents reported unemployment. While a minimal number of respondents have a government job, the remaining work at small shops as a help.

Majority of the families are engaged in occupations highly vulnerable to the shifting economic paradigm. As a result, 37 per cent of the respondents lost their jobs, 27 per cent received a salary cut or earned less money due to the economic slowdown. 76 per cent of the respondents who are unemployed are willing to change their occupation due to dearth of employment opportunities in the post-COVID world and for the need to feed their families.

Even while seeking new job opportunities, 38 per cent respondents reported that they have to produce COVID negative reports to the employer, which has added to their ordeals because of lack of testing facilities, knowledge and awareness among the community members, and additional financial burden it imposes. Amongst those who lost their jobs, only 35 per cent respondents hope to find employment in the next 2 months. Out of those who retained their jobs during the pandemic, 52 per cent did not receive any assistance from their employer/workplace, 22 per cent received a salary cut, 16 per cent received assistance for ration, and other helps while only 10 per cent received regular salary as per pre-COVID terms.

The uncertainty around employment and the ability to meet basic needs has a substantial bearing on mental health of the families. 34 per cent respondents felt hopeless and 18 per cent experienced general anger and frustration while 19 per cent were victims to anger of their family members. The respondents also reported to have experienced loss/gain of appetite and stress.

Education

The data shows that 79 per cent of the surveyed families have school going children, where 57 per cent of these students are girls and 43 per cent boys. The distribution of school attending children shows a varying trend across various levels of education. The number of school going children shows a decrease of 5 per cent from primary to secondary education but there is a decrease as high as 26 per cent for the number of girls enrolled at primary level and an increase of 29 per cent in the number of boys. The reason for decrease in number of girls at secondary level can be attributed to various underlying reasons that affect the education of children in these communities. The promotion from primary to secondary education coincides with the changing bodily needs of girls as they hit puberty. The stigma and downgraded narrative around menstruation leads to various parents dropping out their girl child from schools.

There is a steep fall in the number of children enrolled for senior secondary education, representing a difference of 78 per cent with respect to the enrolment at secondary level. The number of students enrolled for senior secondary education accounts to 68 per cent and 87 per cent less for girls and boys, respectively. The enrolment of girls for secondary education is low as child marriages are prevalent in these communities. Most of the girls are married at the age 16-18 and boys start looking for jobs with local vendors, shops or labour work to support their families. The communities' inclination towards higher education of children is also impacted by lack of opportunities, awareness, and financial ability among others. Enrolment for university/college education is mere 6 per cent as compared to primary education enrolment of children in these communities.

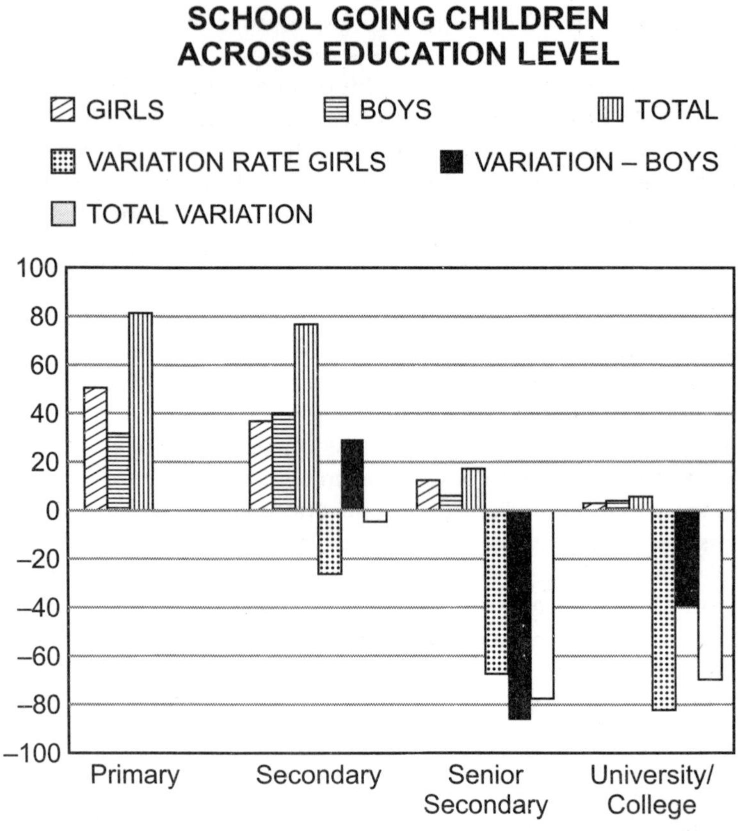

School going children across education level

Families with school-going children reported 54 per cent awareness regarding the conduct of online classes by the institutions. Unavailability of smart phone/laptop/internet (75%) was reported as primary reason for lack of awareness/knowledge about online classes. The families also reported that despite the availability of a smart phone at home, the time bound access to live classes poses a problem for children to join their classes and continue their education, where only 46 per cent families reported that their children are attending regular classes. More than 60 per cent of the families reported that no assistance was provided by the school for ensuring access to online classes and regular attendance of students. 59 per cent families confirmed that their children are finding it difficult to focus and understand their syllabus through online classes. Out of this 60 per cent, 35 per cent families confirmed that they are unable to assist and help their children in studies, the children being the first generation learners. 32 per cent families said that they don't have enough resources (like smart phones or internet) to support their children for online classes and 15 per cent said that the family person who can help in the studies are out and working, making it difficult to help the children in the studies.

The outbreak of COVID-19 and shutting down of schools to contain the virus has impacted the studies of the students. 47 per cent of families feel that the school won't be able to complete the entire syllabus which would impact the learning of children. 31 per cent families fear that children's education might stop because of the challenges to understand the online classes and lack of resources. 11 per cent fear that the college admissions and further studies might be affected, and 7 per cent of them believe that the education of few children might stop, especially the girls.

Suggestions

- **Improved community outreach** – The failure of the state to provide adequate assistance and play a better role in mitigating the impact of COVID-19 was primarily due to lack of community outreach and the contextual understanding of the varied problems unique to such communities. The state needs to play a vital role in ensuring better community outreach in order to understand the impact of such emergencies on the marginalised and high-risk communities. This shall provide insights and foresight for adequate planning. Rigorous data collection and profiling can further help the state in planning specific interventions in the future.
- **Beneficiary targeting** – The government schemes meant to reach the poor of poorest are impacted by major exclusion error, leading to poor targeting of public resources and

inadequate state assistance during such emergencies. The impact of exclusion and lack of state outreach has been observed in the study with communities depending on civic and philanthropic organisations for ration and food.

- **Enhanced social security and social protection** – The government's efforts for providing social security to the vulnerable communities are primarily characterised by mere contingent interventions instead of proactive planning and active social security and protections. There is a need for more focused and targeted interventions to ensure economic safety and security, especially for the socio-economic marginalised groups.
- **Support to the caregivers at home** – For ensuring uninterrupted learning and smooth adjustment to the radically transformed educational experience, the schools and the faculty needs to support the caregivers who are helping children learn while the schools are closed. The efforts should be complimented by providing the required operational support with regards to digital classes by ensuring access to smartphones, tablets and computers through engagement with the district/state authorities and civic organisations.
- **Access to healthcare** – The need to improve the health infrastructure and access to proper medical care has been highlighted by the pandemic but the focus remains on multi-speciality and large hospitals, often inaccessible due to reluctance, lack of awareness, the time consuming nature of appointments and diagnosis. The further improvement of the healthcare infrastructure needs to be made much more inclusive through a larger outreach of the government hospitals and clinics to the grass-root level. The spotlight currently centred around just the physical well-being has led to ignorance of the mental health issues in such communities, therefore, the healthcare needs to be more inclusive to ensure the overall well-being.

Conclusion

The COVID-19 crisis has put the spotlight on the conditions of daily wage migrant workers/people from unorganised sector. From major salary cuts to the absence of income because of the lockdown, people had to cut down on their daily consumption of food. Even with the accessibility of ration through government's Public Distribution Shops, families struggled to get enough food and sometimes skipped their meals because of the limited accessibility and more mouths to feed.

Many individuals, government shops and NGOs had an important role to play in supporting these households during the lockdown. However, the community people still struggle with no employment and salary cuts making it inadequate for them to continue supporting their families. In such complicated times with so much of uncertainty, families have experienced stress, anxiety and other mental health issues that led to the increase in discord, fights and violence in the household.

The families struggled to manage resources for the online classes of their children and hence impacting the studies of the children. The lockdown not only impacted the studies of the children (from regular one-on-one interactions to online classes) but also their routine and interaction with their peers. Many parents reported that they fear their child's education will be hampered, especially the girls'.

Equal efforts by civil society organisations and government is needed to strengthen the support to people especially from the socio-economically marginalised communities to create more employment opportunities, distribution of food supplies and health kits to families with no income, awareness around the online classes and special support to children who are first generation learners. Schools can also take a lead in providing extra help to students finding it difficult to cope up with their studies, providing study materials and also providing services of the counsellors.

References

Laxman, Manjula. (2020), *COVID-19 Pandemic Impact on Marginalised Groups in India,* Lecture delivered on Online Faculty Development Programme-Workshop on Applied Economics, Dept. of Economics, C.U. Shah University & ISM Patna, 14/07/2020.

Mahler, Gerzon, Daniel, Lakner Christoph, Andres, R., Aguilar Castanede & Wu Haoyu. (2020), *Updated Estimates of the Impact of Cvid-19 on Global Poverty*. World Bank Blog. 8/06/2020.

Hussmanns, Ralf. (2004), *Measuring the Informal Economy from Employment in the Informal Sector to Informal Employment*. Policy Integration Department Bureau of Statistics, International Labour Office, Geneva.

Mehrotra, Santosh, and Jajati K. Parida. (2019), *India's Employment Crisis: Rising Education Levels and Falling Non-agricultural Job Growth*. Centre for Sustainable Employment, Azim Premji University.

15

Domestic Violence against Women in India during Lockdown: A Content Analysis

Winnie Joyce A., Ms. Anns Mariya, Ms. Archana, Ms. Gigin Mariya, Ms. Irin Theresa and *Ms. Shemi Saji*

Introduction

In our society, family is considered as the most important thing. Family is defined as a group consisting of parents and their children living together as a unit. Every family have facing some kind of issues for example financial issues, addiction, job loss etc., one of the most danger issues in family is "Domestic violence". Domestic violence is increased now a days.

Violence is not only the physical, it included emotional, spiritual, mental, sexual, social and economic. Domestic violence is dangerous behaviour of a person. The domestic violence is not only happening by the husband it may be done by any family members. Women are most victims of the domestic violence. In all-over South Africa has highest statistics of gender-based violence in the world.

Domestic violence may be a global issue across national boundaries also as socio-economic, cultural, and racial. This problem isn't only extensively discrete geographically, but its occurrence is very widespread, making it a distinctive and accepted behaviours. Domestic violence is profoundly ingrained and has profound effects on the health and well-being of women. The continued presence is undependable morally. The cost to people, health services, and society is immense. Yet no other major problem of public health has been so widely ignored than little understood.

Domestic violence may be a sort of abuse that happens within the house, between relations or couples and family. A male offender and a female victim, frequently his wife or girl friend, are the traditional picture of abuse. There are also female perpetrators of abuse, however, and males are also victims. Any violence perpetrated against another by any family or part of a family can qualify.

Domestic violence can take many forms: property loss, psychological and emotional abuse, physical abuse are the common forms. On the trivial but still quite serious side, culprits of violence may impend victims or use verbal put-downs and a bad name, plan to widely degrade them, or play manipulative mind games. Abusers could also act very jealously, and work to regulate victims' access to family and friends or employment. The abuse could also be life-threatening enough so that the victim loses employment due to diminished output while at work, or is prevented from performing at all.

In its most violent form, violence will involve actual physical and sexual violence, the kidnapping of youngsters, torture or murder of pets, etc. Some victims are driven to suicide. Studies have shown that if someone is living with domestic violence, they can cause physical, emotional, social, and psychological loss to children and young people as anxiety, depression, emotional instability, eating disorders as well as sleeping disorders. While men and women are both affected but, 76 per cent of women are the victims according to the department of justice.

Types of Abuse

1. Physical abuse

Physical abuse is one of the domestic violence. Physical aggression includes kicking, biting, slapping, beating, shoving, pushing, pulling hair, smoking, slashing, pinching, physical aggression is a body contact injury to another human. Sexual abuse is also included in this. Sexual maltreatment happens when the victimizer constrains or endeavours to pressure the casualty into having sexual contact or sexual conduct without the casualty's assent. This regularly appears as conjugal assault, assaulting sexual body parts, actual viciousness that is trailed by constraining sex, explicitly belittling the person in question, or in any event, making sexual quips at the casualty's cost.

2. Emotional abuse

In this includes negating or collapsing the casualty's self-appreciation worth as well as confidence. Psychological mistreatment frequently appears as consistent analysis, ridiculing, harming the casualty's relationship with his/her kids, or meddling with the casualty's capacities.

3. Economic abuse

It happens when the victimizer makes or attempts to make the casualty monetarily dependent. Monetary victimizers frequently look to keep up absolute authority over money related assets, retain the casualties' admittance to reserves, or restrict the casualty from going to class or work.

4. Psychological abuse

It is non-physical acts agents' partner or family members. It includes mental issues the partner threatening or hurt himself/ herself, mood changes emotional issues etc. The most psychological abuse is hidden injuries. It targets the partner thoughts, feelings emotional. Domestic violence prevalence is one of the top health issues that concerns in the country. It is a kind of abuse that in some cases, abusers may not even understand that they are inflicting domestic violence on someone else. On the other hand, victims may not take action against their abusers. If they don't understand that the behaviour, they're experiencing is indeed domestic violence.

It is also critical that the families and loved ones of the victims be in a safer position to intervene if they realize what domestic abuse looks like. It is also crucial that people consider the concept of domestic violence and the different forms it can take.

According to the U.S. Department of Justice Office on Violence against Women, the concept of domestic violence is a form of assault. Also important is that friends and loved ones of victims are in a better place to help if they understand what domestic violence looks like. Therefore, it is important that people understand the definition of domestic violence and the many forms it can take.

Objectives of the Study

1. To understand the ratio of domestic violence against women in India.
2. To know the types of abuse against women in India.
3. To understand the age group is mostly affected.

Data Collection

This study adopted secondary source of data collection happened against women in the month of July, August, September, October, November 2020 from various newspapers and online sites.

Results & Discussion

Domestic violence cases against women are found and reported by different newspapers.

S.No.	Date	Age	Location	Cause of Incident	Religion	Consequence Faced by the Family
1	June-2	24	Ludhiana	Woman set herself on fire at her house	Hindu	As the victim is 80% burnt, it was really difficult for the family to recognize.
2	June-3	22	Jaipur	Woman commit suicide after fight with husband. (Dowry death)	Hindu	The family filed the case against victim's husband and family.
3	June-4	28	Hyderabad	Pregnant woman ends her life over harassment.	Hindu	The case was registered by the police. Family members are against the victim's husband.
4	Sep-5	25	Delhi	Physical abuse from in-laws	Brahmin	Due to financial crunch due to lockdown, family lost everything. Woman filed case against the victim's husband for abusing her.
5	Sep-13	23	Patna	Mistreatment by her husband and in-laws on several occasions.	Hindu	Victims' family filed case against the husband and his mother. She moved to her brothers' place.
6	Oct-5	19	Uttar Pradesh	Gang rape	Dalit-Hindu	Family members were not allowed to see her body and not to be present at the cremation.

7	Nov-3	23	Bhopal	Domestic Violence against her husband	Dalit-Hindu	Due to global pandemic they lost their job and the family fell into great debt.
8	Nov-30	28	Gujarat Ahmedabad	Brahmin woman file case against in-laws for forcing her to embrace Jainism	Hindu	Due to intercaste marriage father in-law and mother in-law started harassing her to follow Jainism.
9	Dec-13	22	Hyderabad	US citizen booked for triple Talaq on Hyderabad.	Muslim	He stayed with her about five months and he promised to Talaq.

Table 15.1: Distribution table of the age which the domestic violence against cases reported

Age	No. of cases	Percentage
19 to 22	2	22
23 to 26	5	55.55
27 to 30	2	22
Total No. of Cases	9	100

Table 15.1 shows the age of the domestic violence against case reported during the month of June to December. The majority of the domestic violence reported among the age of 19 to 30 years and the least among the age of below.

Table 15.2: Distribution table of the places in which the domestic violence cases mostly reported

Places	No. of Cases	Percentage
Delhi	1	11.11
Gujarat	1	11.11
Hyderabad	2	22.22
Ludhiana	1	11.11
Jaipur	1	11.11
Patna	1	11.11
Bhopal	1	11.11
Uttar Pradesh	1	11.11
Total No. of Cases	**9**	**100**

Table 15.2 shows the places where domestic violence cases mostly reported. The majority of the domestic violence cases reported in Hyderabad which is 22.22 per cent and total number

of cases reported from June to December in all the places is 9 and the average of the domestic violence cases is 11.11 per cent.

Table 15.3: Distribution table of the religions in which domestic violence case against women are reported

Religion	No.of cases	Percentage
Hindu	8	88.88
Muslim	1	11.11
Total No. of Cases	**9**	**100**

Table 15.3 shows the religion in which domestic violence case against reported during the month of June to December. The majority of the domestic violence reported in Hindu religion is 8 cases which is 88.88 per cent. In Muslim religion, the total number of cases reported is 1 which is 11.11 per cent. The total number of cases reported in these respected religions is 9.

Table 15.4: Domestic violence cases in the month of June, September, October, November and December 2020

Month	No.of cases	Percentage
June	3	33.33
September	2	22.22
October	1	11.11
November	2	22.22
December	1	11.11
Total No. of Cases	**9**	**100**

Table 15.4 shows the percentage of number of cases reported in the newspaper during the month of June, September, October, November, December. The majority of cases reported in the first three months, i.e., ratio of 33.33. There is a small variation in the month of December (0.09%).

Table 15.5: Distribution table of the type of incident which the domestic violence cases reported

Type of incident	No of cases	Percentage
Suicidal	3	33.33
Physical abuse	2	22.22
Gang rape	1	11.11
Mental torturing	2	22.22
Total	**8**	**100**

Table 15.5 shows the categorization of which type of incident reported during the month of June, December. 33.33 per cent is the suicidal cases reported, physical abuse 22.22 per cent and 11.11 per cent are gang rape and 22.22 per cent are reported as mental torturing cases. No other type of incidents reported during the specific month.

Indian women filed more domestic abuse cases during the first process of lockdown than reported in the last 10 years in a comparable period. But even this unusual spurt is just the tip of the iceberg, as 86 per cent of abusive women in India do not seek aid. The study shows that the domestic violence against the women is mainly of the age group of 19 to early thirty-sixth also signifies that the importance of safety and security that should be given to her husband's house as well. Many women get abuses from her husband and in-laws. The women are not safe even in their house. Financial crisis due to global pandemic put the families into greater debt. Many people who depend on daily wages, lost their job and hope. The physical and mental issues faced by the women from their husband and in-laws are the first reason for all this domestic violence. Even this violence led them to suicidal attempts also. Experts claimed that lockdown period really made them to financial crisis and the people who depends on daily wages lost all the hopes in their life and thus it creates domestic quarrels. Domestic abuse is often witnessed in low-income rural households, but women living in urban areas are also no exceptions.

With the closure of offices and schools amid the lockdown, many couples are going through difficulties in their relationship, which escalate to verbal abuse and physical violence. Sandeep Ojha, state head of an NGO based in Paliparan colony, pointed out that women suffered the most–emotionally and physically–amid any crisis. "The COVID crisis has led to tons of tension in many households such as job losses, bankruptcy and family disputes. As a result, many men are venting out their frustration on the women in the family", he said and added that the pandemic had highlighted the importance of uplifting women at the grass-root level.

Conclusion

From the review of research females in between the age to be more likely to be the victim of domestic violence. By examining the location of the incident most of the violence issues are reported from northern part of the nation. The victims are mostly from Hindu religion. The consequences faced by the family differ from case to case. But in overall view husband's family is not treating the victim well as well as from the spouses. Different kinds of exploitations are faced by the females as many of them are treated as slaves who are tied tightly under the marriage knot as they are lacking freedom to enjoy the outer world. Poor mental and physical health also causes these youth to be the victims of the violence. Lack of education is also the reason behind most of the issues from rural areas of the nation. Women empowerment can help these youth to escape from these dilemmas to an extent as they can enable themselves to stand on her own foot in the world.

References

Barter, C., McCarry, M., Berridge, D. et al. (2009). *Partner exploitation and violence in teenage intimate relationships*. London: NSPCC.

Bowen, E., Heron, J., Waylen, A. et al. (2005). Domestic violence risk during and after pregnancy: findings from a British longitudinal study. *BJOG: An International Journal of Obstetrics and Gynaecology*, 112: 1083-9.

Brandon, J., Hafez, S. (2008). *Crimes of the community – honour-based violence in the UK*. London: Centre for Social Cohesion.

Brandon, M., Sidebotham, P., Bailey, S. et al. (2012). "New learning from serious case reviews: a two year report for 2009-11". London: Department for Education.

Devine, A., Spencer, A., Eldridge, S. et al. (2010). "Cost-effectiveness of Identification and Referral to Improve Safety (IRIS), a domestic violence training and support programme for primary care: a modelling study based on a randomised controlled trial." BMJ Open access.

Dick, S. (2008). "Homophobic hate crime: The Gay British Crime Survey." London: Stonewall.

Donovan, C., Hester, M., Holmes, J. et al. (2006). Comparing domestic abuse in same sex and heterosexual relationships [online]

Feder, G., Ramsay, J., Dunne, D. et al. (2009). "How far does screening women for domestic (partner) violence in different health-care settings meet criteria for a screening programme? Systematic reviews of nine UK National Screening Committee criteria." *Health Technology Assessment*, 13 (16).

Hester, M., Westmarland, N. (2005). *Tackling domestic violence: effective interventions and approaches*. London: Home Office Research, Development and Statistics Directorate.

Holt, S., Buckley, H., Whelan, S. (2008). "The impact of exposure to domestic violence on children and young people: a review of the literature." *Child Abuse and Neglect*, 32: 797-810.

16

Pandemic and the Household: The Changing Dynamics of 'Home' as a Social Institution during COVID-19

Shilpi Sikha Das

Introduction

The unprecedented outbreak and continuous spread of the virus from 2019 resulted in enforcing physical distance, and homestay in a nationwide lockdown. With the shutdown of all social institutions, the family became the central institution that keeps functioning and was expected to keep other institutions running. Social institutions are mechanisms or patterns of social order focused on meeting social needs. Jonathan Turner defines social institutions as, "a complex of positions, roles, norms, and values lodged in particular types of social structures and organizing relatively stable patterns of human activity concerning fundamental problems in producing life-sustaining resources, in reproducing individuals, and in sustaining viable societal structures within a given environment" (Turner, 1997). According to Anthony Giddens, "Institutions are the more enduring features of social life which refer to institutional orders, modes of discourse, political institutions, economic institutions, as well as legal institutions" (Giddens, 1984). Institutions are the embodiment of designated social structures for carrying out different tasks which are guided by different rules.

The five major social institutions are politics, religion, economy, education, and family. The incidence and distribution of the virus have been at a rampant speed which made all the institutions dysfunctional. Family is the smallest and intimate social institution that has been functioning without any pause. Family is the basic unit of society that creates space for other institutions to function. Murdock defines family as, "a social group characterized by common residence, economic co-operation and reproduction. It includes adults of both sexes, at least two of whom maintain a socially approved sexual relationship and one or more (own or adopted) of the sexually cohabiting adults" (G.P. Murdock, 1949). The household was seen to be a "living arrangement" for a family unit. In 1997, Haralombus and Herald defined family as, "a procedure for socialization, economic activity and sexual activities that consists of two persons of the opposite gender" (1997). Contemporary times have witnessed a change of traditionally defined family. Evolution of human and the society have had an impact on the dimension in family structure and family's designated roles. The pandemic further questioned the family as an institution and highlighted more of the household as an emerging social institution. Household unlike family is not marked by blood relatives or kinship, household is a common space for individuals or family who live together. Though, household and family are seen to be used synonymously; the pandemic lockdown has provided an opportunity in differentiating both.

The composition of household in the modern society has been changing. A household can comprise of flatmate, roommate, live-in partner, or rented out to individuals or families that might not be biologically or socially connected. The only thing in a household can be sharing a common roof, where sharing a common kitchen is not always necessary. The sudden nationwide lockdown imposed restriction on travel and made it difficult for people to travel home. The "Stay-at-Home" mantra was impeached upon human conscience with the outbreak of the virus through all possible mediums. The lockdown forced people to run for shelter, either by travelling back to their hometown or by finding a secure place to survive. Even without family, the household started functioning that has been fulfilling the needs and demands of the individual, family, and community.

The chapter aims to understand the changing dynamics of the household during the pandemic; which includes three main themes:

(a) The role of the household during the pandemic.

(b) The demand from the household and the services provided.

(c) The change in traditionally gendered norms of household and division of labour.

The household not only provided shelter during the pandemic and lockdown but was also expected to provide food security, education, and space for employment and productivity. It is important to note that even the makeshift and temporary settlements have been active households in this period of crisis. The role of the household in providing services against the needs and demands of the society and other social institutions are discussed below thematically:

1. **"Work-From-Home" (WFH):** The pandemic introduced us to a new normal where the household space turned into offices and workstations. Advance technology and the digital world have provided the opportunity of telecommuting and remote working possible without a confined space. While for the IT and related sector shifting to "Work-From-Home" has been relatively easier than many other sectors, where shifting to WFH has not been a smooth transition. According to International Labour Organization (ILO), WFH is a working arrangement in which a worker fulfils the essential responsibilities of his/her job while remaining at home and by using Information and Communications Technology (ICT). This arrangement helps in ensuring employment as well as continuity of work. As per ILO data, around 68 per cent of the world's total workforce that includes 81 per cent of employers have been recommended or are required workplace closures (2020). The employers and workers must be practical, flexible, and sensible of the present environment and each other. The current temporary WFH arrangements make the workers and employers take care of their own physical and mental health and also abide by rules to ensure productivity.

The basic requirements of WFH in the present time include a computer or laptop and even mobile phones with uninterrupted network and electricity connectivity, a workspace that can be used for 6-9 hours (or even more) without any disturbance, enough natural daylight, water and sanitation facility, etc. The household has been responsible for providing such a workable environment. Before the pandemic, WFH was convenient and with the pandemic, it became a necessity. A range of positive benefits has been associated with working from home, especially during the pandemic which includes reducing risks and being safe at home, improved family and work integration, reduction in fatigue, improved productivity, and flexibility of work. On the other hand, a few studies have listed out the challenges faced by the employees both in terms of mental and physical well-being. The blurring of the physical and the organizational boundaries between work and home have had a negative impact on employees. Extended hours of work, more time in virtual environments, lack of social and emotional interaction are common concerns raised. Physical and emotional discomfort that was mentioned includes stress, anxiety, depression, insomnia, eating disorders, fatigue, body pain, etc. (Oakman, Kinsman, Stuckey, Graham, & Weale, 2020). The issue of adjusting to the new work environment, self-efficacy, and structuring have been highlighted during this period, where a good percentage of overall productivity is dependent on technology. The need for tools, equipment, and other facilities to WFH has been added to the household expenses.

2. **Online education:** As all levels of educational institutions were closed during the pandemic, online education became the only mode of the functional institution. The household became the facilitator of online education. The pedagogical shift from the traditional method to the modern approach of teaching-learning has been a journey from the classroom, labs, field works to Zoom calls, webinars, Google meets, online conferences, etc. Just like Work-From-Home (WFH), online teaching and learning are also completely dependent on technology which required a workspace, electronic device, electricity, uninterrupted working hours, etc. This global crisis needed innovative changes to suit the need of the hour that involves both internal and external changes. The famous change model by Kurt Lewin (1958), the three-step process—unfreezing,

changing, and refreezing can be used to analyze and understand the change in the teaching-learning world. The unforeseen circumstances due to COVID-19 have resulted in unfreezing of the traditional teaching-learning process. Thus, to prevent any disturbance in the educational system, an online mode of education was used to make the educational institutions function. The need and motivation to change and restructure for continuity of an institution during the pandemic also depends on the stakeholders of the institutions. Here, the two important institutions are the educational institution and the household.

Online education has been beneficial for many as it provided opportunities to take up different courses online which might not be feasible during the institutional framework. It also provided opportunities to attend international collaborative projects/ seminars/conferences that would otherwise economically difficult for many students and scholars. On the other hand, online education also brought about different barriers to education.

3. **Health and well-being:** With the lockdown and surge of the pandemic, healthcare services are prioritized for COVID-19. The human resource, infrastructure, and healthcare service delivery were channelized to flatten the wave of the pandemic. "Home" became the designated space to maintain well-being and health during the pandemic. World Health Organization emphasizes physical activity, healthy eating, looking after our mental health, healthy parenting, and quitting tobacco as major areas to remain "Healthy at Home". The major factors of maintaining health and well-being at home can be discussed as follows:

3.1 Physical activity: Physical activity plays an important role in preventing and controlling various lifestyle diseases. Sedimentary conditions increase the risk of cardiovascular diseases that includes obesity, hypertension, diabetes, metabolic syndrome, etc. According to Narici et al. (2021), inactivity during confinement during lockdown can result in a reduction in maximum oxygen consumption level, oxygen absorption capacity, and cardiac volume. Reduction in VO_2 max and the absorption capacity of O_2 are associated with a higher mortality rate. In addition, this decrease affects blood circulation and the oxidative function of the muscles. Being physically active not only helps to reduce body mass and prevent cardiovascular diseases, but it also helps to improve immunity and cope with viral diseases. A narrative review was done with 876 articles from five major databases: PubMed, SCOPUS, SPORTDiscuss, and Web of Science (WoS). Initially, a total of 1312 articles were selected that were published until the 14th of May, 2020, and 876 were taken for the study. Four recommendations are found to be common across all the articles on physical activity during the pandemic that includes (Polero, et al., 2021):

- Aerobic physical activity recommendations.
- Strength training recommendations.
- Recommendations for flexibility, stretching, relaxation, and meditation.
- Recommendations for balancing activity.

WHO recommends the amount and nature of physical activity at home as mentioned below (WHO, 2020):

Age group	Activities
Infants under 1 year of age	• All infants should be physically active several times of the day. • For those not yet able to move, activities should include at least 30 minutes in prone condition (tummy time), as floor-based play, that can be spread throughout the day while awake.
Children under 5 years of age	• All young children should spend at least 180 minutes a day in a variety of activities at any intensity. • Children of the age group of 3-4 years should spend at least 60 minutes of this time in moderate to vigorous-intensity physical activity.
Children and adolescent of the age group of 5-17 years	• All children and adolescents should be active for at least 60 minutes a day of moderate to vigorous-intensity physical activity. • This should include activities that strengthen muscles, bones and should be done at least for 3 days per week. • Doing more than 60 minutes of physical activity daily will provide additional health benefits.

Adults aged over 18 years	• All adults should do at least 150 minutes of moderate-intensity physical activity throughout the week, or at least 75 minutes of vigorous-intensity physical activity throughout the week. • For additional health benefits, adults should increase their moderate-intensity physical activity to 300 minutes per week, or equivalent. • For developing and maintaining musculoskeletal health, muscle-strengthening activities involving major muscle groups should be done on 2 or more days a week. • In addition, older adults with poor mobility should do physical activity to enhance balance and prevent falls on 3 or more days per week.

The existing double burden of diseases in India has been further pressed upon by the pandemic that increases the risk of non-communicable lifestyle diseases and mental health conditions. The lockdown has resulted in overeating, stress eating, not enough physical activity for calorie burning, change in the sleep cycle, etc, which increases the risk of non-communicable diseases and low immunity. Co-morbid conditions compromise the health and well-being of individuals that further increases COVID complications (Rawat, Dixit, Gulati, Gulati, & Gulati, 2021).

3.2 Healthy Diet: Even before the lockdown, the household has always been responsible to ensure food and nutritional security for the members of the household. Food and nutritional security can only be achieved when, "people at all times, have physical and economic access to sufficient, safe and nutritious food that meets their dietary needs and food preferences for an active and healthy life" (Report of World Food Summit, 1996). According to United Nations System Standing Committee on Nutrition (2020), the four distinctive dimensions of food security are the physical availability of food, economic and physical access to food, food utilization, and the stability of these three dimensions. The pandemic has disrupted the supply chain that resulted in wastage of food and increased the ratio of unmet needs (Singh, 2021). Both external and internal factors have affected the food and nutritional security in the community. The external factors include the availability of food that is affordable and are not controlled for profit-making markets and regulations. The available food should be accessible to the people that are satisfactory in quality and quantity. The internal factors include desirability, accessibility, affordability, and good quality to ensure healthy consumption patterns.

With the lockdown household and the caregivers become more responsible in ensuring food for the members. The gender inequality of food and nutritional security is another challenge in the pandemic. According to the "The State of Food Security and Nutrition in the World, 2020" report, 189.2 million people are undernourished in India. These accounts for 14 per cent of the population, also 51.4 per cent of the reproductive age group of 15-49 years are anemic. India bears the burden of 34.7 per cent of stunted children under the age of five years and 20 per cent of wasting. The cases of malnutrition-related diarrhea, pneumonia deaths are high in the country. Women face greater challenges in getting access to productive resources, services, technologies, market, financial assets than men, the disruption in the networks have created further vulnerability to the socio-economic lives of women. The nutritional and supplement programmes have been severely affected in the lockdown which has left pregnant women, lactating mothers, adolescents without nutritional and supplementary support. With less amount of food in the household, women are often seen to compromise on their share of food, which has intensified during the pandemic with more scarcity of food and increasing cost of food (Gendered Impact of COVID-19 and equitable policy responses in agriculture, food security, and nutrition, 2020). The imbalance in internal and external factors results in higher levels of malnutrition and food insecurity thus, failing to achieve sustainable food security goals. With the existing low nutritional status of the country, uneven food security statistics across the country, and disruption in the supply chain for over, India is expected to face serious food and nutritional security implications in the coming time which needs urgent attention and intervention.

3.3 **Mental Health:** The unpredicted chaos that the pandemic has put the human population into caused stress, tension, anxiety, anger, denial, and panic. The lockdown has pushed people to hardships that are beyond imagination. Loss of employment, loss of shelter, losing people to the pandemic, confinement, are very few triggers that have seriously affected the mental well-being of people. Large-scale disasters have often resulted in a significant negative impact on individuals resulting in depression, post-traumatic stress disorder, domestic violence, substance abuse, behavioural disorder, child abuse, eating disorder, sleep disorder, etc, which is also seen during the pandemic (Das, 2020). According to Roy et al. (2020), the most vulnerable population of mental health during the pandemic are children, geriatric population, frontline workers, migrant workers, people who tested positive of COVID-19, survived or family members of COVID-19 patients, and people with existing mental health illness. The shift to an online mode of education, Work-From-Home, has created anxiety, stress, and adjustment problems both for the children and parents in the household. The rise in reported suicide cases during the pandemic grabbed national and international attention. Panigrahi et al. (2021) conducted a content review of reported cases of COVID-19 related suicide cases. A total of 1856 articles were selected from 1632 newspaper articles and 224 reports of television channels. Out of which 151 cases were selected for the study which was collected from 1st February, 2020 to 30th September, 2020. The study found that 35.7 per cent of cases were recorded in institutional settings, 13.9 per cent of suicide happened at home, 9.9 per cent cases near to home, and 40.3 per cent deaths occurred in hotels, railway tracks, well, etc. The major causes were fear, the stigma of contamination, misconception related to COVID-19. The lockdown also prevented physical interaction, social support, and any other form of collective/social engagement causing a monotonous uncertain life.

4. **Security:** The household has been responsible for ensuring the safety and security of the members during the pandemic.

Unfortunately, India witnessed the highest record of 1477 recorded cases of domestic violence from the period of 25th March, 2020 to 21st May, 2020 which has been the highest compared to the last 10 years (Radhakrishnan, Sen, & Singaravelu, 2020). The chances of violence against women and children have drastically increased with the abuser and victim sharing more time in confined space, increase in household stress, also with the additional condition of economic or job loss, the risk of violence escalates (Usher, Bhullar, Durkin, Gyamfi, & Jackson, 2020). The structural gender inequalities at different levels of society, political crises, socio-economic instability triggers violence in the household. Using the Routine Activity Theory (RAT), Krishnakumar and Verma (2021) categorized three components of domestic violence. The three components are motivated offender, a suitable target, and absence of a capable guardian. In most reported cases, the motivation of the perpetrator was alcohol and unemployment, the suitable target is generally women and children in the household as they are considered the lower inertia, visible, and are easy access to vent out anger and frustration. Restriction of movement during the lockdown took away the social support system, law and order have been diverted to pandemic control which gives the perpetrator more space and time for violent actions and behaviour. Cases of physical abuse, assaults, attacks were also recorded upon tenants by landowners during the lockdown.

The household has been burdened with all the functions of major social institutions with leaving no space for negotiation during the lockdown. It is also important to note that basic needs of survival: food and clothing have been possible only with shelter during the pandemic, as 1.77 million population are homeless in India. Thus, the shelter has been a social privilege where each household experienced different challenges during the lockdown. The options of WFH for people who belonged to mainly skilled employment, in the same way online education was only feasible for students—a teacher with electricity, electronic devices that excluded differently-abled students and teachers. The lack of space in the household makes physical activity and home isolation a challenge in the Indian scenario.

Conclusion

The pandemic has changed the "normal functioning" of society and the deconstructed social institutions. COVID-19 is a systemic human development crisis that has unveiled the existing loopholes that existed through inequality, injustice, and power division. The structural disparity that has existed through the years has only escalated to the worse during the pandemic. The basic needs of survival: food, cloth, and shelter become a challenge for the majority of the population in India who lives hand-to-mouth. Unemployment and under-employment have created economic unrest in the household. The present COVID lockdown has been considered to be the second fatal economic distress after the "Great Depression". Long term economic constrains in the household increases the risk of drop-out from educational institutions, higher level of gender nutritional insecurity, compromised well-being and health, and violence. Maintaining a healthy environment for work, education, productivity, physical and mental well-being, emotional and social support was also superimposed on the household which added extreme burden on caregiving. Women who are traditionally considered as caregivers in the household have been fighting an unrecognized and unacknowledged struggle to meet the food security and well-being of each member of the household. To equate the equilibrium of the household, the pandemic has taught us the importance of gender sensitivity, equality in the household. Putting all the responsibility on one member of the household will affect the functioning and environment of the household which is the only secure space during the lockdown. Only the end of the pandemic will reveal if the emergence of the household as a social institution is permanent or temporary.

References

#HealthyAtHome- Physical Activity. (2020). Retrieved from World Health Organization: https://www.who.int/news-room/campaigns/connecting-the-world-to-combat-coronavirus/healthyathome/healthyathome---physical-activity

(2020). An Employer's guide on working from home in response to the outbreak of COVID-19. International Labour Organization.

Das, S. (2020). "Mental Health and Psychosocial aspects of COVID-19 in India: The Challenges and response." Journal of Health Management, Vol. 22, Issue 2, 197-205.

(2020). Food Environments in the COVID-19 pandemic—Impact of positive policy actions to deliver sustainable healthy diets for all. United Nations System Standing Committee on Nutrition.

G.P. Murdock. (1949). Social Structure. New York: Macmillan.

(2020). Gendered Impact of COVID-19 and equitable policy responses in agriculture, food security, and nutrition. Rome: Food and Agriculture Organization of United Nations.

Giddens, A. (1984). The Constitution of Society: Outline of the Theory of Structuration. Cambridge: Polity Press.

Haralombus , M., & Herald, R.M. (1997). Sociology: Themes and Perspectives. Collins.

Krishnakumar, A., & Verma, S. (2021). "Understanding Domestic Violence in India During COVID-19: a Routine Activity Approach." Asian Journal of Criminology, 16, 19-35.

Lewin, K. (1958). "Group Decision and Social Change." In E. E. Maccoby, T.M. Newcomb, & E.L. Hartley, Readings in Social Psychology, 3rd Edition (pp. 197-211). Rinehart and Winston, Holt.

Narici, M., Vito, G., Franchi, M., Paoli, A., Moro, T., Marcolin, G., . . . Maganaris, C. (2021). "Impact of sedentarism due to the COVID-19 home confinement on neuromuscular, cardiovascular and metabolic health: physical and pathological implications and recommendations for physical and nutritional countermeasures." European Journal of Sports Science, April 21(4), 614-635.

Oakman, J., Kinsman, N., Stuckey, R., Graham, M., & Weale, V. (2020). "A Rapid review of mental and physical health effects of working at home: how do we optimize health." BMC Public Health. 20. 1825.

Panigrahi, M., Pattnaik, J.I., Padhy, S.K., Menon, V., Patra, S., Rina, K., . . . Patro, B. (2021). "COVID-19 and suicides in India: A pilot study of reports in the media and scientific literature." Asian Journal of Psychiatry, March, 57.

Polero, P., Seco, C. R., Adsuar, J. C., Gomez, J. P., Ramos, J. R., Redondo, F. M., . . . Vivas, J.C. (2021). "Physical Activity Recommendations during COVID-19: Narrative Review." International Journal of Environmental Research and Public Health, 18.65, 1-24.

Radhakrishnan, V., Sen, S., & Singaravelu, N. (2020, June 24). Domestic violence complaints at a 10 year high during COVID-19 lockdown. Retrieved from *The Hindu*: https://www.thehindu.com/data/data-domestic-violence-complaints-at-a-10-year-high-during-covid-19-lockdown/article31885001.ece

Rawat, D., Dixit, V., Gulati, S., Gulati, S., & Gulati, A. (2021). "Impact of COVID-19 outbreak on lifestyle behaviour: A review of studies published in India." Diabetes and Metabolic Syndrome, 15(1), 331-336.

(1996). Report of World Food Summit. Food and Agriculture Organization of the United Nations (FAO). Retrieved from: http://www.fao.org/3/w3548e/w3548e00.html

Roy, A., Singh, A.K., Mishra, S., Chinnadurai, A., Mitra, A., & Bakshi, O. (2020). "Mental Health Implications of COVID-19 pandemic and its response in India." International Journal of Social Psychiatry.

Singh, D. (15 May, 2021). "Hunger and food security in the times of COVID-19." Journal of Social and Economic Development. Retrieved from https://link.springer.com/content/pdf/10.1007/s40847-020-00124-y.pdf

Turner, J. (1997). The Institutional Order. New York: Longman.

Usher, K., Bhullar, N., Durkin, J., Gyamfi, N., & Jackson, D. (2020). "Family Violence and COVID-19: increased vulnerability and reduced options for support." International Journal of Mental Health and Nursing, Vol. 29 (4), 549-552.

17
Impact of COVID-19 on Women's Life: A Study

Somodatta Bhattacharjee

Introduction

With the outbreak of the COVID-19 pandemic, life has been chaotic for more than a year and the situation has not changed a bit. Now we all are trying our best to embrace the 'New Normal'. But in this new normal, something has not changed at all and that is the violence on women. Corona virus is not only a medical issue but one that is both a social and economic case. And when it has a socio-economic side associated to it, this is very important to identify and understand the phenomena and in what ways it has its impact on gender. There is serious gendered impact of the ongoing pandemic. Though the crisis has its impact on both men and women in different ways and not necessarily in the same direction but it affects women much more. And that is because of the social structure of our society. Women are subjected to unrealistic and unachievable personal and professional demands and expectation to run everything smoothly as if nothing abnormal has happened and anything otherwise would subject them to violence.

Objectives

The primary objectives of this study are to address issues like—

- To inquire into the detrimental impact of pandemic-lockdown on women;
- To analyse the possibilities that has developed out of the situation; and
- To suggest some changes in policies to tackle the situation.

Methodology

The present study is based on various reports of International Monetary Fund (IMF), International Labour Organisation (ILO), World Health Organisation (WHO), and United Nations (UN), articles published in many journals, websites and many leading daily newspaper reports.

COVID-19 Pandemic and its Impact on Women

The first objective of the study has been divided into three sections like difficulties faced by women in job, violence on women and health issues faced by them during the time.

Difficulties of Women in Work during Pandemic-Lockdown

The pandemic has been extremely tough on job sector and economy in many different ways. ILO has estimated that full or partial lockdown measures across the globe has affected 2.7 billion workers representing around 81 per cent of world's workforce (Nations, 2020). According to IMF; the total unemployment rate was 23 per cent in the month of April-May, 2020, but in June, it came down to 11 per cent (Kalita). Apparently it looks positive that once in June when the unlocking had started; people started getting back to their work. But what is the number of women who got their job back in the month of June is a serious matter. According to a report published by UNO, in many countries the first round of layoffs has been particularly hit the service sectors like hospitality, tourism where women employees were significantly high in number. From the past experiences and the data we have right now, it is not very difficult to assume that due to COVID-19 there is going to be a substantial downward moving slope in women's income which will further force them to live in acute poverty.

So far as women working in the formal sector are concerned, the unusual pandemic situation put a lot of extra burden on them. Considering the lockdown and the absence of domestic help, women have to handle and juggle with both personal and professional life. Since everyone has been working from home, the ideal 9-5 working hours cease to exists. Many stakeholders of formal sector have laid off their workforce. In such situation, the existing and additional work pressure has been distributed amongst the available workforce. Here lies the problem. During the pandemic and the resultant lockdown, in a family, men can work exclusively on their office assignment but women are expected to handle both the office and home. In actuality this is responsible for further worsening the situation for women. Under such immense pressure of holding both personal and professional lives together, she has to deliver her work on time. But if she fails, there comes the severe pressure and problem of job security. There is visible and remarkable imbalance in the gender distribution of unpaid care work. Before the pandemic, women used three times as much unpaid care and domestic work as men. And now when there is global pandemic women have to do a lot more of it in addition to have equal amount of workload as men.

According to some rough statistics, 40 per cent of working women work as part-time worker compared to just 13 per cent men who work part-time (National Webinar on India's War Against COVID-19: Approach and Gender Dynamics). So women who work as part-time are likely to be earning less and sometimes belong to the informal sector lose their job easily. Reason for their joblessness in the pandemic period also finds its echo in the fact that it is believed in their family that since they are earning less and not able to support the family financially in a very stable way, so it is wise for them to leave the job and take full care of the family members in the difficult time. Also there are reports which indicate that during this pandemic and lockdown, the productivity of professional and working women in terms of research, publication has gone down heavily as women being burdened with household work. Many women had to learn technologies to take online classes, to take part in webinars and others. This creates a lot of anxiety and stress for some while many others are not able to come up with new ideas, concepts in their work at the same pace as their male counterparts.

In the field of developing and emerging economies, informal sector is the largest amongst them in India. It has been estimated that amongst 90 per cent of India's labour force work in the informal sector and among women who work, more than 90 per cent work in the informal economy (Overcoming Precarity: How Informal Women Workers coped during COVID-19). These women workers work mostly as *beedi* rollers or helpers at some local industry and others. Naturally, they have limited access to formal sources of credit or lack in bargaining skills and ended up losing their job in the wake of pandemic and lockdown.

In the informal sector, domestic helpers, caregivers are mostly women. About 70 per cent of women are working in this sector and their jobs are less secured and also they earn less (ILO). During the lockdown and even after it, their employers are not calling them back and they are struggling to get a fresh employment regardless of their precautionary measures. People are under the fear of coming into the contact of the virus and thus they do not seek any domestic help from outside. The condition of the women workers in the informal sector gets even more precarious because they are neither protected by any association of their own nor they can afford to have any legal support. Though the Central and the State governments in India have started many initiatives like Unorganized Workers' Social Security Act (2008), Contract Labour (Regulation and Abolition Act), 1970 and others to address the vulnerability. But none of these efforts could bring in any change due to the unawareness of the workers regarding the very existence of these Acts. And the situation now is even more complicated when the nation is under the grip of the fear of virus infection, the helpless, jobless women workers nowhere else to go to understand and fight for their right.

Violence against Women during Pandemic-Lockdown

Domestic violence is one of the common forms of violence against women and the lockdown has intensified that to an alarming level. It is found that in 2017, 87,000 women who died globally were actually killed by intimate partners or family members (United Nations Office on Drugs and Crime, 2019). On 6th April, 2020, Antonio Guterres called for a ceasefire to deal with the 'horrifying' global surge in domestic violence (EPW, 2020).

Home is unfortunately not safe for everyone. Women's lack of autonomy in the patriarchal homes is making them more vulnerable and to abuse and violence. Women are beaten up, threatened by their husbands. Uncertain period of quarantine has propagated anxiety and depression in people. There are cases where wives are tortured, beaten up by their alcoholic husbands for not getting alcohol. These examples are conclusive of the fact that gender violence is nothing but it happens due to the desire to establish the power and power-relationship in the family. The uncertainty of financial stability also resulted in an increase of violence against women. Due to pandemic, support services are also struggling. Police, judiciary and health services which are the primary responders are overwhelmed. Civil society's help is also absent due to the lockdown.

The leading daily newspapers of the country are constantly reporting about the increasing cases of violence against women. News of domestic violence was coming from almost all the corners of the country. On 26th April, 2020, news was published in the *Hindustan Times* describing, in Kerala, a member of the State Women's Commission received a call from Chennai pleading for help by a man saying her sister and her daughter are hiding in a forest as her husband hurled both of them out of the house. Later, the case was investigated and the husband was taken into custody. This is just one case but there are hundreds of thousands of cases happening everyday.

The complaints for violence at home had been doubled within a month in the initial days of nationwide lockdown. In the first week of March, the complaints were 30 in number but by the last week, the number became 69. To combat the situation, National Commission for Women has launched a WhatsApp number for the victims so that they can seek help more easily. (COVID-19). But in a country like India where 57 per cent of women do not have access to phone or do not have a personal phone, it is of limited use to even have a special WhatsApp number to make the process to lodge a complaint against the violence. In the home isolation during lockdown, when it is evident that women have no other support at their disposal and cannot escape easily, violence against them takes a serious turn.

UN Secretary General Antonio Guterres is of the opinion that "COVID-19 could reverse the limited progress that has been made on gender equality and women's right."(The indirect impact of COVID-19 on women). The global scenario of violence and abuse against women is a burning example of it. The cases of violence are also mounting up because in our society it is believed that husband is justified to beat his wife if she fails to take care of him or cannot serve him hot food, disobey his orders and others. The National

Family Health Survey Data reveals the data that 42 per cent of men and 52 per cent of women do not consider violence as a crime.

The education of girl child has also faced the brunt of the pandemic. In March, 2020, UNESCO estimated that the pandemic was preventing 1.52 billion children from school. (The indirect impact of COVID-19 on women). This will have a deep and long lasting impact. Out of these 1.52 billion children, some will never make their way back to school due to poverty and being out of education for quite some time especially girls face a heightened risk of female genital mutilation and early marriage. According to the recent report, State of the World Population (SWOP), published by the UNFPA, COVID-19 may increase the already concerning early marriage, violence, and sex birth ratio at birth and others.

Health Issues Faced by Women During Lockdown

The COVID-19 pandemic and the resultant lockdown poses a lot risk on the heath of women and girl, especially if they are in fragile conflict affected areas. Under the pandemic situation, there has been a disruption of critical health, humanitarian and development programmes. Such imbalance in health sector can pose life and death consequences to the pregnant and disabled women.

Malnutrition is very common in developing countries like India. In 2000, a study suggests that nearly 70 per cent of non-pregnant women and 75 per cent of pregnant women suffer from malnutrition and most of them are anaemic in terms of iron deficiency (Navaneetham K., 2008). This makes them more vulnerable to the virus infection. Maximum frontline workers are women. This automatically makes them more vulnerable to the virus infection. Their risk gets doubled because there is a scarcity of PPE kits and where kits are available, they do not fit the women as these are designed and sized based on a male template. Marginalised women are at high risk of many other infectious diseases due to lack of proper sanitation and unhealthy menstruation system. COVID-19 had added more pressure to such unhygienic condition. A survey was conducted by the Menstrual health alliance and it was found that because of lockdown, the accessibility to menstrual hygiene products and clean toilets in the presence of male and older family members has been a challenge to women and girls (Hindu, 2020).

The pandemic has not posed health hazard only but is responsible for serious mental issues of women. People are finding it difficult to maintain sanity and women are the worst hit. Being solely responsible to run a house, look after children and elderly people and handle a job, women are suffering from extreme stress and anxiety. A study was conducted by two researchers of the University of Essex in the month of June and it was found in the study that the number of women suffering from stress, anxiety and loneliness has increased up to 27 per cent during the lockdown (Kalita. A.).

New Opportunities

The pandemic has brought untold miseries to people's lives in general and women's lives in particular. But amidst such crisis, they are trying their best to do well. Women who were employed in the informal sector in the pre-COVID times have involved themselves in making masks. In India almost 19 million masks have been made by 20,000 self-help groups across the country. Also women are taking up the business of sending home cooked meals to the COVID-19 positive patients who are in home isolation.

Suggestions

To minimise the vulnerability faced by women during the pandemic-lockdown, following measures maybe suggested:

- Attempts should be made to include women and women's organisation at the heart of the COVID-19 response;
- Basic social protection should be extended to the informal workers;
- Efforts should be made to build more equal, inclusive and sustainable economy and society through gender responsive policies;
- More intense psychological support should be offered to women and girls to combat the stress and anxiety for having a balance in personal and professional spheres;

- The capacity of shelters for the victims of violence should be extended by repurposing places like hotels and others;
- Informal spaces like grocery, pharmacy and others should be offered to women to lodge their complaint in case of extreme emergency without alerting the perpetrator; and
- Gender neutrality should be introduced to domestic responsibility.

Conclusion

It is a time of uncertainty. Every day we are losing our loved ones to this deadly virus. We have been given some time to spend with our family which is otherwise almost unimaginable. We need to understand and acknowledge the fact that this is a global crisis and we have to face this together. This is the time to stay united, physically distanced and emotionally connected to restrain the cynicism and fight back the virus with all our might.

References

EPW. (2020). "COVID-19, Domestic Abuse and Violence: Where Do Indian Women Stand?" *EPW*. Retrieved May 2021, from https://www.epw.in/engage/article/COVID-19-domestic-abuse-and-violence-where-do

Hindu, T. (2020). *Coronavirus lockdown/Women's access to menstrual hygiene products hit.*

ILO. (n.d.). *https://www.ilo.org/global/publications/books/WCMS_626831/lang--en/index.htm.* Retrieved May 2021, from https://www.ilo.org/global/publications/books/WCMS_626831/lang--en/index.htm

Kalita, A.B. (n.d.). *Women in COVID-19 Pandemic—Some Issues.* Retrieved May 2021, from WOMENINCOVID-19PANDEMIC-SOMEISSUES

(n.d.). *National Webinar on India's War Against COVID-19: Approach and Gender Dynamics.* Retrieved May 2021, from https://www.youtube.com/watch?v=Xud8TYowRPU&t=4045s

Nations, U. (2020). *Policy Brief: The Impact of COVID-19 on Women.* UNO. Retrieved May 2020, from https://www.un.org/sexualviolenceinconflict/wp-content/uploads/2020/06/report/policy-brief-the-impact-of-covid-19-on-women/policy-brief-the-impact-of-covid-19-on-women

Navaneetham, K.J. (2008). "A Factsheet on Women's Malnutrition in India." *Economic and Political Weekly.*

Overcoming Precarity: How Informal Women Workers coped during COVID-19. (n.d.). Retrieved May 2021, from https://www.epw.in/engage/article/overcoming-precarity-how-informal-women-workers

(n.d.). *The indirect impact of COVID-19 on women.* Retrieved May 2021, from https://www.thelancet.com/action/showPdf?pii=S1473-3099%2820%2930568-5

(2019). *United Nations Office on Drugs and Crime.*

18
Stress and Challenges of Parents of Persons with Multiple Disabilities during COVID-19 Pandemic

B. Preethi Meena

Introduction

A major turning point in the life of millions of people around the world took place in the end of 2019, due to COVID-19. It has caused thousands of people to lose their loved ones, watch them struggle helplessly, and leave people in a devastated situation. COVID-19 has not only affected people physically but emotionally as well. India, a country with the second largest population in the world, is struggling in administering the mediation of the severe acute respiratory syndrome. Awareness about the sudden outbreak was raised by The Ministry of Health and Family Welfare. Necessary actions were also taken by the Government of India.

The present situation has led to a bigger and massive challenge in the public health sector, clinical research and practitioners and medical professionals. One among the major vulnerable groups in the community includes people with multiple disabilities who are indeed at a greater risk of being affected by the syndrome. People with multiple disabilities generally fall into the undeserved group when it comes to public health and health research initiatives. The distress experienced by this community impacts the family's emotions, instability and stress.

The COVID-19 introduced additional challenges to the families of adults with Multiple Disabilities. Sudden loss of employment, social isolation were experienced by the families of adults with multiple disabilities. This has led to a situation in which families conduct necessary therapeutic intervention with support from the professionals. A study conducted by C. Neec, R. Fenning et al. (2020) conducted a study on the impact of COVID-19 in the families of children with intellectual and developmental disabilities which stated that parents have reported that looking after their children with the loss of their essential service was one of the major drawbacks. Nevertheless, parents have also stated that this pandemic has resulted in positive changes mainly in keeping the family united and creates a supportive environment.

Review of Literature

Over the years, the concept of disability has been evolved and classified into three different views. They are in terms of medical, social and International Classifications of Functioning, Disability and Impairments formed by the World Health Organization. Disability in terms of medical concept is considered to be impairments due to any severe health conditions or abnormality in an Individual's body or mind. Whereas Disability is referred to as a social construction and purely based on human rights issues. ICF (International Classification of Functioning, Disabilities and Handicaps) combines both the concepts and defines it as a Bio-psychosocial model.

Courtenay, K., B. Perara (2020) highlighted that COVID-19 pandemic has an influence on everybody in society. People with intellectual disabilities (ID) are particularly vulnerable to the pandemic's physical, emotional, and social impact. Hatton and Emerson (2010) in their research, focused on certain psychological insights into how families adapt to new lifestyles. Although there are several psychological causes to explore, one significant field that has been linked to stress is the use of coping mechanisms. However, the latest coronavirus disease pandemic (COVID-19) is affecting society. Changes in the environment, interrupted habits, and limited access to resources and social networks can have a distinct effect on autistic people and their families, contributing to severe regression in others. A research conducted by Min A. Kim, Jaehee Yi et al. (2021) resulted that parents of persons with intellectual disabilities were worried that their adult child was not aware of COVID-19, it was more dangerous as they are vulnerable. Ka- Huen (2020) states that most elderly parents say they don't know how to care for their children with ID during the COVID-19 pandemic because of their own deteriorating physical health and the fear of not knowing how to stay unaffected by it. The imposition of social distancing and isolation interventions as a result of the COVID-19 pandemic is having an additional and unforeseen effect on families. Many people's mental health would most likely be harmed as a result of these policies (Brooks et al., 2020). Assuring that information is available in formats and methods that are specific to the individual with IDD, allowing them to understand the risk of COVID-19 infection, the reason for changes in their lives, and how long these changes can last (Beyond Words, 2020). Dasgupta N. (2020) described that the fight against COVID-19 has been a collaborative effort. And the pandemic's effect on civil society, stakeholders, and non-governmental organizations demonstrates the value of collaboration. Nemțeanu, M.S. and Dabija, D.C. (2020) states that the current COVID-19 pandemic has prompted a rapid response from a slew of non-governmental organizations (NGOs) to provide practical assistance. These efforts demonstrate the importance of non-profit organizations as resource providers and facilitators for various organizations, especially public hospitals.

Objectives of the Study

Following are the objectives of the study:

1. To understand the stress level of parents of persons with multiple disabilities.
2. To understand the different challenges faced by the parents during COVID-19.
3. To understand the remedies and strategies adopted by Diya Foundation to help the parents overcome the challenges during COVID-19.

Research Methodology

The aim of the study is to understand the stress level and challenges faced by parents of persons with multiple disabilities during COVID-19. The present study was conducted in the Silicon Valley of India, Bengaluru, Karnataka also known as a hub of most of the tech companies around the world. It is also known as the Garden city with its year bound blossoms and greenery. Person with Disabilities are often prone to some form of discrimination and exclusion. Even though every individual deserves the same right and opportunity to enjoy their rights, when it comes to people with disabilities there is a huge number who are often neglected and not taken into considerations. The government has implemented many programmes and initiatives to work alongside with the community and NGOs. To understand the difficulties and challenges of parents and how the NGO - Diya Foundation addresses these challenges, has encouraged the researcher to conduct this research. The present study uses convergent parallel dynamic design that includes both qualitative and quantitative elements in the same phase of research method which is created by gathering, analyzing, and presenting collected information. This research design consists of detailed procedure of information that is required to structure the further research. It facilitates smooth functioning of the research process as it has a significant impact on reliability of the outcome of the research.

The study obtains quantitative data of 20 parents of Person with Multiple Disabilities using an online survey. The survey contains details of socio-demographic details of parents, their stress level during the COVID-19. An 18-item self-report scale developed by Berry and Jones in the year 1995 which is used to measure the above aspects of the study. This study also contains a descriptive study of 2 parents by interview method to understand their challenges and analyze the intervention of Diya foundation to resolve their challenges. The researcher obtained Simple Random sampling technique using the purposive method to study the 20 respondents for quantitative data who were informed about the aim and need for the study well in advance and their consent has been recorded. The researcher also used the lottery method to study the two case studies for qualitative data with their consent. Secondary data was also considered for the study by the researcher thus adding to the in-depth understanding of the objective of the study.

Data Analysis

The Parenting stress is a cross-cultural concept and is impacted by specific family and life circumstances. Parenting stress is exacerbated by difficult life circumstances such as poverty, single parenting, and parental separation, but it is mitigated by the inherent benefits of parenting, such as feelings of comfort and affection (Louie, A.D., Cromer, L.D., 2017). The data collected was focused on a thematic analysis and organizing sequentially that includes collection of data, generating the information, reviewing the information and lastly documenting the findings. In this present study, the researcher has used MS Excel to upload the raw data. In order to analyze the uploaded data, the researcher has used IBM SPSS Statistics Version 21 software.

Data Interpretation and Results

Data analysis and interpretation is the process of systematically applying logical methods to describe and evaluate data. It helps to build credibility of the research by giving a theoretical base. It deals with analyzing the data collected and interpretation of the information in detail by using tables, graphs and pie charts. Following are the brief analysis and interpretation of variables used for the study. To understand the nature of the respondent, the researcher collected socio demographic data of the participants.

Chart 01:

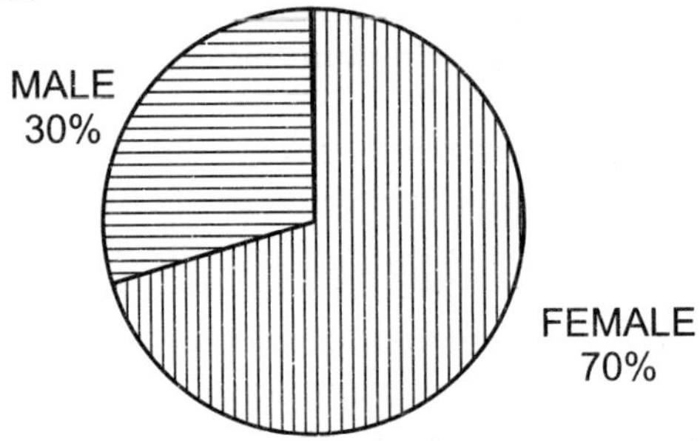

(A) Gender: The research further broke down the sample based on gender. Out of 20 respondents, 14(70%) are female and 6 (30%) are male.

Chart 02:

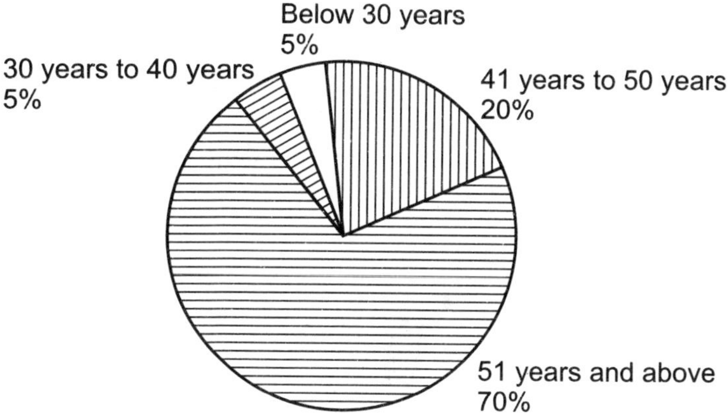

(B) Age: The research studies 4 age groups, i.e., below 30 years (out of 20 respondents—1 (5%), 30 years to 40 years (out of 20 respondents— 1 (5%), 41 years to 50 years (out of 20 respondent–4 (20%) and above 51 years. (out of 20 respondents— 14 (70%).

Chart 03:

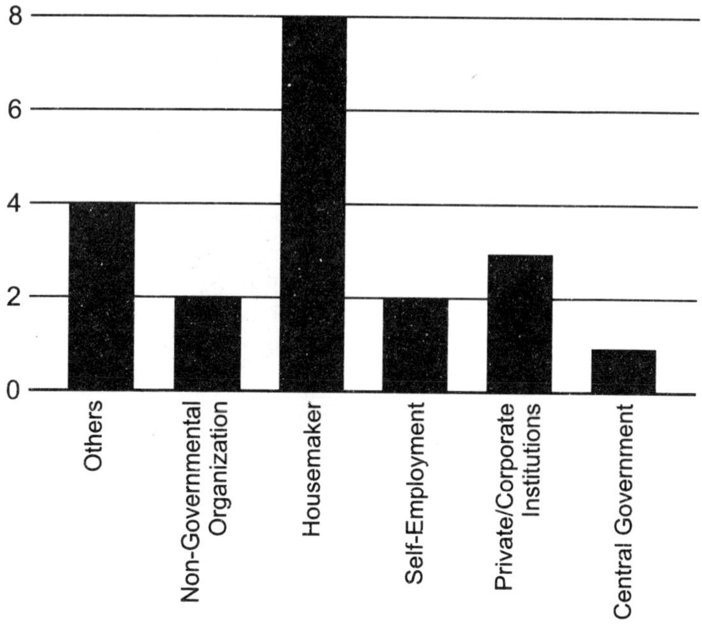

(C) Type of job of the respondents: The respondents varies into different categories namely Central Government employee - out of 20 respondentss -1 (5%), Non-Government employee - out of 20 respondents - 2(10%), Private or corporate employee - out of 20 respondents - 3(15%), Self-employment - out of 20 respondents - 2(10%), Homemaker - out of 20 respondents - 8(40%) and other job - out of 20 respondents - 4(20%).

Chart 04:

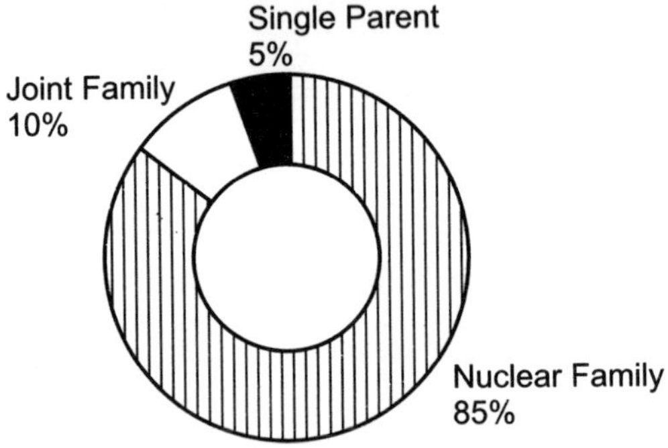

(D) Type of family: The researcher has studied the family type into three categories, i.e., Joint family out of 20 respondents - 2(10%), Nuclear Family out of 20 respondents - 1(5%) and single parent out of 20 respondents - 17(85%).

Chart 05:

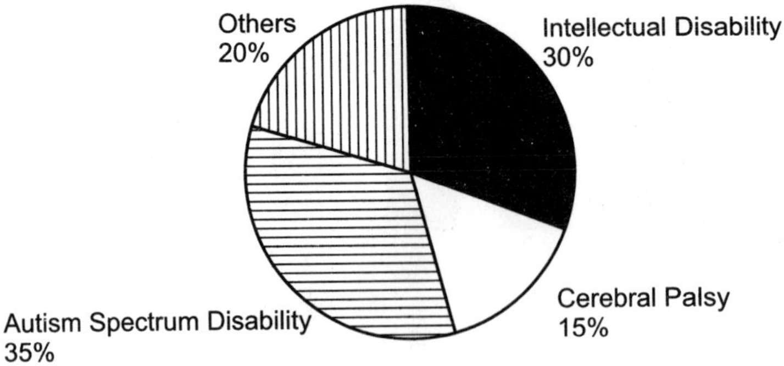

(E) Nature of disability of the respondent's child: The researcher further studied the nature of the disability of the respondent's child into 4 categories namely - Intellectual disability - out of 20 respondents - 6(30%), Cerebral Palsy - out of 20 respondents - 3(15%), Autism spectrum Disability - out of 20 respondents - 7(35%) and other disability - out of 20 respondents - 4(20%).

The researcher also describes parental stress by conducting an online survey. This tool helped in measuring the levels of stress experienced by parents. Also this tool takes into account positive and negative aspects of parenting. It provides a measure that considers positive aspects of parenting as well as the negative, 'stressful' aspects traditionally focused on. The parental stress scale describes feelings and perceptions about the experience of being a parent (respondents). This tool used 5 points (strongly disagree - 1, disagree - 2, undecided - 3, agree - 4 and strongly agree - 5). Although questions 1, 2, 5, 6, 7, 8, 17, 18 were measured as reversed scoring to keep up the credibility of the scoring. Table 18.1 shows that out of 20 respondents (parents of person with multiple disabilities) majority, i.e., 17 parents (85%) fall in the low stress category and 3 respondents i.e. (15%) (Parents of person with multiple disabilities) fall in the high stress category.

Table 18.1: Distribution of parental stress

	Frequency	Per cent	Valid per cent	Cum. per cent
Low stress level	17	85.0	85.0	85.0
High stress level	3	15.0	15.0	15.0
Total	**20**	**100.0**	**100.0**	

Chart 06:

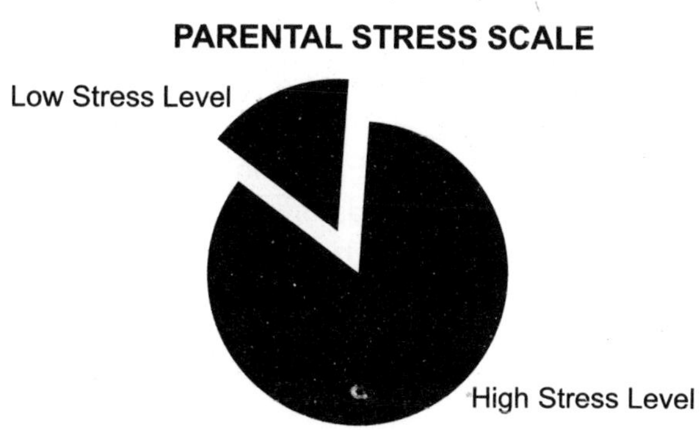

Distribution of low stress and high stress level of parents of persons with multiple disabilities. Out of 20 respondents, 17 parents of persons with multiple disabilities have low stress levels or below average (18 points to 54 points). These parents see this pandemic as a coping mechanism and hope to overcome it soon. Out of 20 respondents, 3 parents of persons with multiple disabilities have high levels of stress or above average (55 points to 90 points). These parents face pressure of not knowing how best to take care of their children with special health needs. They have no idea how to prepare or engage future care planning for their children with multiple disabilities if they become infected or pass away, leaving behind their children, due to the high prevalence of COVID-19.

The researcher also conducted a qualitative study by interviewing 2 parents of persons with multiple disabilities who shared their challenges and how the interventions from Diya Foundation has benefited them during COVID-19 pandemic.

Case Study 1:

Parent (XYZ) aged 67 years who is a retired special educator shares her challenges faced during COVID-19 pandemic and remedies used by Diya Foundation for the benefit of parents and their family " Terrible, I was not able to control my son who has autism. He just couldn't understand why he was not let out, meet his relatives and No more going to Diya for his training. His daily routine was disturbed, no more evening walks. It was a pandemic inside him and that added to the stress in the family. His tantrums increased, shouting at everybody also increased. Moreover, one of his close relatives was tested positive and that broke him completely. We all panicked and felt helpless. My son found it difficult to control his emotions. The entire family felt devastated and lost hope. Meanwhile, Diya Foundation initiated online classes with trainees. Meeting his trainers and friends online was a new experience. For a few weeks, he had a tough time, he requested the trainers to open Diya soon. Dr. Babita the rehabilitation psychologist and Ms. Padma the trainer worked closely with him. They conducted online counselling sessions, exercises to calm him down, assigned activities to keep him busy at home, spending quality time with his family and most importantly made him understand the pandemic situation, importance of taking precautions and sanitizing. Gradually, he was able to respond positively. He started reading the newspaper and understood the current situation of COVID-19. With the regular online classes (daily living skills, cooking, personal social skills and employment training) his tantrums reduced, he started calming down, he engaged himself in household work, made healthy salads, poha, etc. Diya also provided online physiotherapy for my son and that helps him to stay fit and strong. The happy hour sessions that take place once in a week have helped him a lot. In this session, trainees like him join and the trainers conduct fun activities, recreational sessions and this keeps them united and together.

Diya Foundation felt the need of connecting with parents and supporting them during this difficult time. They conduct family sessions every week in which parents join on google meet and discuss their challenges and find solutions. Each parent shares their remedies and strategies on how to tackle the situations. Some parents also share some of the best practices and parenting tips. This motivated the other parents to execute the best practices in their family. It was peer learning. In the beginning parents came with a lot of complaints on different behavioural issues of their child, but now the parents are coming up with more solutions and methods. Diya' intervention has helped us a lot. There were so many positive changes I could encounter in my son especially during the pandemic. Before he used to give orders to us but now he listens to us and it's a two way communication. He is aware of the situation outside and doesn't compel to go out every day. He takes turns in responding back. I even lost hope and was tired but Diya didn't give up. It was because of Diya's intervention that I am at peace now and my emotional state is better. I can see a future for my son in this competitive world. Get to know meeting was organized in which the trainers and parents got to know what works for my son, what does not work, his support system, what is important and what is not, his goals and routine. All of these have resulted in a positive response at my home. We all feel united and are a support for each other."

Case Study 2:

Parent (ABC) aged 57 years who is currently working as a special educator shares "During the lockdown, one challenge was keeping my daughter occupied. This challenge was mostly during the initial days. Later on, she found out her own ways of keeping herself occupied, she kept herself occupied by watching educational videos on her laptop, listening to music on the balcony, playing music and dancing. She doesn't like to sit in one place, she will sit for some time, walk around, listen to songs on the balcony, etc. Once in a while, when she is in the mood she will help at home, rolling the *chapatti* or *puri* for the whole family. She also hangs the clothes and folds the clothes. Another challenge was she wanted to go out earlier but now she is okay to stay at home. As a family we tried to keep her occupied by giving her a timetable to follow. But it was difficult for me as I had to manage my job as well, I had my work and my classes. So I gave up and let her be by herself. She figured out how to keep herself occupied and that was the best thing for me. She does what she likes to do each day, according to her own time and pace. She is not comfortable with a set routine or a routine given according to time, she likes to do things on her own time and pace. She will finish the tasks given on that particular day but on her own time; she doesn't like to be forced which may lead to upset moods and me being stressed. During the lockdown, the online classes being implemented by Diya Foundation were a huge help. With the online classes in place, her morning routine is set—she can get up and finish her tasks in order to be ready for the classes. In the afternoons, she does whatever she likes to do. During the offline classes, before the lockdown, her routine at Diya was a huge help, especially that she was engaged in something (tasks/classes) from 9 am-4:30 pm everyday. She was engaged with constructive activities and being occupied with offline classes. Her trainer Ms. Jerusha has provided a routine for her self-monitoring tool, a chart that tracks her activities on a daily basis that includes household work, leisure activities, etc. and has opened up different avenues for her to work on something as simple as cutting her vegetables. Her personal trainer also worked closely with her thus helping her in all possible ways. This time of COVID has helped the family become closer to each other and act as a support structure for each other. Major positive changes I witnessed as a mother was that my daughter has become extremely social and very expressive in the sessions—shares whatever happens in the day with her family. And as a mother, it's been supportive and stress free because I am able to learn a lot through the family sessions that are conducted on a regular basis via online. This platform gives me so much insight about how to tackle any challenge and it surely proves the success of the collective."

Limitations of the Study

Following are the limitations of the study by the researcher:

1. This study contains small sample size, i.e., 20 parents of persons with multiple disabilities and hence the findings of this study cannot be generalized.
2. As this study was conducted only in Bengaluru city, the findings may not be applicable to other parts of the country.

Future Scope

Following are the future scope of this study:

1. In future, the researcher could conduct a comparative study that tries to understand the stress level of various groups - parents of lower age group and parents of older age group.
2. The researcher could conduct a study on understanding the emotional well-being among the parents.

Suggestions

In the light of this study, the researcher provides the following suggestions:

(*A*) *Government, Society and Family:* Family and society should support people with multiple disabilities by treating them as one of their priorities even during emergency cases and most importantly be supportive to them physically and emotionally. Even though there are various schemes and programmes to benefit the persons with multiple disabilities and their families, the effectiveness of it must be duly measured. Mainstreaming them in society is itself a big support to them. Governments can connect with organizations who promote best practices during the crisis like this pandemic and encourage their services.

(*B*) *Non-Government Sectors and Community based organizations:* The vision and mission of the organizations can also benefit the families of the target group and thus building a stronger society that looks at people as a valued member in the society, promoting inclusion and leading a dignified life. NGOs and community based organizations can tie up with similar organizations and share the remedies, best practices and interventions. They can also conduct research in the effectiveness of these interventions.

Conclusion

The research highlighted that the majority of the sample falls under low stress level, i.e., 17 parents and the rest, i.e., 3 parents fall under high stress level. The reasons could differ as there are various variables that could affect the stress level. The intervention of Diya Foundation, who benefit one of the vulnerable group, i.e., Persons with Multiple Disabilities and their families act as possible remedies and strategies that can empower and benefit similar interest groups in society. Apparently some of the parents started seeing a positive impact of the COVID-19 in terms of being supportive to each other, understanding each other better and most importantly being sustainable and empowering themselves as they begin to address the challenges of their child. In the beginning of COVID-19, the parents expected certain challenges in their child's life such as changing in a daily routine, isolation, regression in skills, feeling bored, lack of physical activities and increased behavioural challenges. But now, they have drawn different strategies to tackle the challenges in the family. This pandemic has encouraged all members to take active participation in the family and understand each other better. With the training and support from Diya Foundation towards the families, parents stated that the professional aid has reduced their stress, built their confidence and be hopeful.

Acknowledgement

I would like to acknowledge the numerous help and support provided by all the people around me to complete this study successfully. My sincere gratitude to Ms. Maria Santamaria, CEO of Diya Foundation for her encouragement and guidance. My sentimental thanks to Dr. Babita Gupta, Rehabilitation Psychologist for her unfailing support and other trainers as well. A special mention to Ms. Anurupa and Ms. Sadguna.

References

Beyond words, (2020). *Good days and bad days*. London, UK: Author. Retrieved from https://booksbeyondwords.co.uk/coping-with-coronavirus

Brooks, S.K., Webster, R.K., Smith, L.E., Woodland, L., Wessely, S., Greenberg, N. and Rubin, G.J. (2020). "The psychological impact of quarantine and how to reduce it: Rapid review of the evidence." *Lancet* (London, England), 395, 912–920.

C. Neec, R. Fenning et al. (2020). "Examining the impact of COVID-19 in ethnically diverse families with young children with intellectual and developmental disabilities." *Journal of Intellectual Disability Research,* https://doi.org/10.1111/jir.12769

Courtenay, K. and Perera, B. (2020). "COVID-19 and people with intellectual disability: impacts of a pandemic." *Irish Journal of Psychological Medicine, 37*(3), 231-236. https://doi.org/10.1017/ipm.2020.45.

Dasgupta N. (2020). "The role of NGOs – Ensuring commitment to social responsibility amidst the COVID-19 pandemic." *The Times of India,* https://timesofindia.indiatimes.com/blogs/voices/the-role-of-ngos-ensuring-commitment-to-social-responsibility-amidst-the-covid-19-pandemic/

Hatton, C. and Emerson, E. (2010). "The development of a shortened 'ways of coping' questionnaire for use with direct care staff in learning disability services." *Mental Handicap Research*, 8, 237–251.https://www.thehansindia.com/hans/opinion/news-analysis/the-role-of-ngos-in-combating-covid-19-pandemic-674577

Ka-Huen. (2020). "Ageing parents of children with intellectual disabilities during the COVID-19 epidemic in Hong Kong." *Public Health in Practice, Volume 1,* https://doi.org/10.1016/j.puhip.2020.100053

Louie, A.D., Cromer, L.D., Berry, J.O. (2017). "Assessing Parenting Stress: Review of the Use and Interpretation of the Parental Stress Scale." *The Family Journal*. *25*(4):359-367. Doi:10.1177/1066480717731347

Min A. Kim, Jaehee Yi et al. (2021). "A qualitative study on parents' concerns about adult children with intellectual disabilities amid the COVID-19 pandemic in South Korea." *Journal of Applied Research in Intellectual Disabilities,* https://doi.org/10.1111/jar.12875

Nemțeanu, M.S. and Dabija, D.C., (2020). "Best Practices of Non-governmental Organisations in Combating COVID-19." In: R. Pamfilie, V. Dinu, L. Tăchiciu, D. Pleșea, C. Vasiliu eds. 6th BASIQ International Conference on New Trends in Sustainable Business and Consumption. Messina, Italy, 4-6 June 2020. Bucharest: ASE, pp. 626-633.

Index